CONFI...

AND RELIGION

The Age of Reason, edited by the outstanding teacher and author, Stuart Hampshire, presents selections from the basic writings of such great 17th century philosophers as Descartes, Leibniz, Spinoza and others, with a penetrating introduction and interpretive commentary illuminating their works.

The 17th century was the great formative era of modern philosophy, marked by the decline of medieval conceptions of knowledge, by the rise of the physical sciences and by the gradual transition from Latin to French and English as instruments of philosophical thought. In this "age of reason," philosophers began to explain natural processes in mathematical terms. They also developed vital concepts of knowledge and certainty, appearance and reality, freedom and necessity, mind and matter, deduction and experiment.

STUART HAMPSHIRE is a Fellow of All Souls College, Oxford. He is the author of SPINOZA, and FREEDOM OF THE INDIVIDUAL.

The Mentor Philosophers

THE AGE OF REASON

The 17th Century Philosophers

SELECTED, WITH INTRODUCTION AND INTERPRETIVE
COMMENTARY

by

STUART HAMPSHIRE

A MERIDIAN CLASSIC

NEW AMERICAN LIBRARY

NEW YORK AND SCARBOROUGH, ONTARIO

© 1956 BY STUART HAMPSHIRE

All rights reserved

MERIDIAN CLASSIC TRADEMARK REG. U.S. PAT. OFF. AND FOREIGN COUNTRIES
REGISTERED TRADEMARK—MARCA REGISTRADA
HECHO EN WINNIPEG, CANADA

SIGNET, SIGNET CLASSIC, MENTOR, PLUME, MERIDIAN AND NAL
BOOKS are published *in the United States* by
New American Library,
1633 Broadway, New York, New York 10019,
in Canada by New American Library of Canada Limited,
81 Mack Avenue, Scarborough, Ontario, M1L 1M8

First Meridian Classic Printing, 1984

1 2 3 4 5 6 7 8 9

PRINTED IN CANADA

Foreword

GREAT PHILOSOPHERS MUST BE READ WHOLE IF THEY ARE
to be fully understood. This is particularly true of systematic thinkers like Spinoza. This book is designed solely as
an introduction to the philosophy of the seventeenth century. It may encourage readers to turn to the original works
themselves.

The following works need to be read in their entirety by
anyone who wishes to go further in understanding the permanent contribution of that century to philosophy:

Hobbes's *Leviathan;* of Descartes, the *Discourse on
Method,* the *Six Meditations,* the *Replies to Objections;* of
Spinoza, the *Ethics, On the Correction of the Understanding, Letters;* of Leibniz, the *Discourse on Metaphysics,*
the *Letters to Arnauld,* the *New Essays on the Human
Understanding,* the Clarke-Leibniz *Correspondence,* the
Monadology, Of the Ultimate Origin of Things.

Of the great commentators, Bertrand Russell's *The
Philosophy of Leibniz* should also be read, together with
the early chapters of A. N. Whitehead's *Science and the
Modern World.*

These are the still-living classics which every student of
philosophy needs to read before he speculates on philosophy himself. Some of the following extracts—but not
many—illustrate rather the development of thought than
surviving problems; most of them illustrate issues which
are still discussed, even if the problems would no longer
be stated in the same way. Much has been omitted, particularly from the works named above, which is still of
living philosophical importance and omitted solely for reasons of space.

The translations of Descartes, Pascal, Spinoza and Leibniz are the responsibility of the editor. Several existing
translations have been used for comparison. The following have been found particularly useful: the Everyman

(Dent) edition of Descartes; the Hale White and Amelia Stirling translation of Spinoza's *Ethics* (Oxford University Press); *Selections from Leibniz*, edited by Professor Philip Wiener (Scribner). Acknowledgment is also due to Mr. A. C. Crombie for the selection from Galileo, which is taken from his *From Augustine to Galileo* (The Cresset Press).

I am indebted for help in the preparation of this book to Mr. Isaiah Berlin of All Souls College, Oxford, and to Mr. B. A. O. Williams, of New College, Oxford.

Contents

Contents

Introduction

PHILOSOPHY IS A CONTINUOUS ACTIVITY OF THE HUMAN
mind, and the divisions between historical periods are always to some extent arbitrary and unreal. But the phase
which can be constructed by beginning with Galileo (1564-
1642) and ending with Leibniz (1646-1716) has a certain unity; it is the great formative period of modern philosophy. It marks the rise of the physical sciences and the
continuing, and almost final, decline of medieval conceptions of knowledge, based upon Aristotelian methods.
Throughout the sixteenth century human reason had, in
different places and in different subjects, asserted its independence of authority and challenged scholastic methods
of thought. But in the sixteenth century the idiom—the
style, the way in which men's minds moved and expressed
themselves—was still that of the old world, and not of our
own; even in reading Machiavelli, Erasmus and Montaigne,
one is aware always of a certain quaintness, as it seems to
us now, which constitutes a barrier between us and them.
Their canons of relevance, their constant appeals to the
authority of ancient Greece or Rome, are not natural to us;
their sense of literalness, and their manner of argument, are
not ours. Most important of all, the national languages had
not yet established themselves, in any form familiar to us, as
the natural instruments of abstract thought. All through the
seventeenth century one can observe the gradual transition
from Latin to French and English as the natural instruments of philosophical thought. At the beginning of the
century Latin is still the unavoidable vernacular of the
learned world; individuals even of genius, such as Bacon
and later Hobbes, seem to be struggling against the poetical
and concrete temperament of their language when they
turn to abstract argument in English; the path of argument

11

from one expression to another has not yet been made
smooth by centuries of use, as it has when they fall back
into Latin. It is for this reason, among others, that Descartes (1596-1650) is normally and properly taken as the
first great modern philosopher, the first of the line which
continues unbroken until the present day. He invented a
style of abstract argument which was clear and simple and
largely free from the technicalities of scholastic Latin.
Philosophy became a proper part of French literature, and
the French language itself was to become the focus of
European civilization.

Philosophy is a free inquiry into the limits of human
knowledge and into the most general categories applicable
to experience and reality. The condition of philosophy at
any time depends in the main upon two related, but
distinguishable, activities of the human mind: religious
and moral belief, on the one hand, and the search for positive knowledge, on the other. When religious belief is firmly
established and largely unchallenged, narrow limits will
be set to the free inquiry which is philosophy; where there
is insecurity or conflict of religious and moral belief, philosophical problems will present themselves with particular
urgency and be left more open to free inquiry. The seventeenth century was an age of religious conflict, in which
Christian theology had often to be defended, in one of its
many forms, with savage desperation; the doctrinal unity
of Western Europe had disappeared, and every thinking
man was aware of this change. At the same time the search
for positive knowledge seemed to be entering on a new
phase with a new vitality; great new areas of natural knowledge had been opened up by Galileo, Copernicus, Kepler,
and many others. It gradually became clear that natural
processes must be explained by laws of nature expressed
in quantitative terms; the key to the understanding of
nature seemed to be found in the application of mathematics
and in precise methods of measurement. The Aristotelian
conception of nature as a system or hierarchy of natural
kinds, distinguished by essential qualitative differences, began to seem inadequate; and yet the logic which had for
centuries been taught in all the schools of Europe still

depended on this conception of nature. It was the logic of the syllogism, which made classification seem the typical subject of argument and the standard expression of knowledge. "All Xs are Ys; this is an X; therefore this is a Y"— this scheme of argument had for centuries been taken as the model of rational inference in the sciences. The sciences were required to arrive at definitions which state the essence and essential properties of things of different kinds. Definition and essence, substance and attribute, essential properties and accidental properties—these are the central notions of scholastic philosophy, ultimately derived from Aristotle.

If the natural order is to be understood as God's museum of things and creatures, eternally divided into their kinds, these are indeed the notions appropriate to the organization of natural knowledge. But if nature is to be understood as the manifestation of mathematically precise natural laws, this logic becomes inappropriate and too narrow; the divisions into kinds by perceived qualitative differences become irrelevant and have no important place in the organization of scientific knowledge. A logic is needed which shows the forms of mathematical argument, since natural knowledge must, as far as possible, assume the form of mathematical demonstration. Natural science must, as far as possible, be abstract and general and indifferent to qualitative distinctions. Laws of motion and change provide a rational explanation of phenomena only if they are stated in the most general terms possible; ideally, they should apply not merely to things of a particular kind. qualitatively distinguished, but throughout the physical realm without restriction. Therefore metaphysicians are led to represent the subject to which natural laws apply as a single, qualitatively undifferentiated substance, called Matter or Extension; all qualitative changes are to be explained as fundamentally changes of state within the single system of material or extended things; the qualitative differences apparent to the human senses are irrelevant to the true understanding of the motions of material things.

Some variant of this view of nature, and of natural knowledge, will be found in Descartes, Spinoza, and Leibniz,

who are the great philosophers of the century. All of them
agreed in rejecting much of the Aristotelian logic still taught
in the schools as being irrelevant to modern scientific conceptions of the world. All of them agreed in rejecting our
ordinary judgments of perception, and the vocabulary in
which they are expressed, as inadequate to the representation of reality. They all agreed that the propositions of the
new mathematical physics more nearly correspond to the
ultimate constituents of nature. But they differed among
themselves in the positive account which they gave of the
ultimate constitution of reality.

It must be remembered that, until the death of Newton
and even later, there was no generally recognized, clear
line of distinction between philosophy and the natural
sciences; "natural philosophy" was the common term
which could embrace both what we would call metaphysics
and what we would call physics. Descartes and Leibniz
were not only philosophers in the narrow, modern sense;
they were also distinguished figures in the history of mathematics and of science. It was part of the function of metaphysical philosophy to suggest the forms of explanation and
system of concepts which scientific investigators of nature
should use. Particularly in the works of Descartes and
Leibniz, the problems of theoretical physics, as we should
describe them, are intertwined with perennial philosophical
problems. Descartes, Spinoza and Leibniz each made his
own suggestions about the nature of space and the fundamental constitution of bodies. Reading them now, we may
choose to disregard those parts of their theories which now
fall within the domain of the experimental sciences; at
least in part, their theories will seem outmoded science, and
we shall be interested only in their treatment of the perennial philosophical problems; these are the problems which
cannot be treated as experimental problems and cannot
fall under any of the special sciences. But we must allow
for, and understand, their motives in constructing a natural
philosophy which was largely speculative but which was
not at that time useless.

Philosophy has always been wider than natural philosophy and more than the philosophy of science. All great phi-

losophers have tried to provide an account, not only of the natural order, but of man's place in nature. A theory of human knowledge and its limits must also carry implications about human purposes and human ends; and a theory of the natural order must also suggest some answer to the problems of creation, and therefore carry some implications about the existence and nature of God. It was in the seventeenth century that the modern conflict, or apparent conflict, between science and religion had its beginning. Galileo was condemned by the Church for disproving the official Aristotelian theories of the motion of bodies. Copernicus and Kepler had discovered the true nature of the solar system, and the whole medieval Christian cosmology was left without a basis. The earth had been shown not to be the center of creation, but, in terms of physical space, an utterly insignificant part of it. This discovery did not immediately become known to educated people in general; it was at first confined to a narrow circle of natural philosophers, many of whom, including Bacon, rejected it. But it was clear that if it did become known, and if it could not be rejected on any rational grounds, popular Christian thought, and the imagery and conception of the world that everyone took for granted, would finally be undermined. The effects would pass far beyond the learned world and would be felt by every educated man, however little he might be interested in science. He would have to think about the place of man in creation in a quite different way. Copernicus' result, like Galileo's, was condemned by the Church, but it was plain that the truth could not be suppressed for long. Two great Christian thinkers had some more or less permanently effective answer to the challenge: Pascal and Descartes. Pascal was not, in the strict sense of the word, a philosopher, and is therefore represented only by two short fragments in this book. He did not try to give a coherent account of the possible range of human knowledge or of the natural order, or even of the moral duties of man. Rather he showed in his *Lettres Provinciales* and in the *Pensées*, what the attitude of Christian faith must be, when men realize, as they should, that none of the ultimate philosophical questions can be answered by human reason; as Mon-

taigne had suggested, there can be no reasonable certainty
in human knowledge; Pascal had looked for, and found, a
desperate moral certainty of the truth of the Christian reve-
lation. The universe is vast and men are physically insignificant within it. Their greatness is that they alone have souls
and can recognize their own insufficiency and their dependence on God. Pascal was a skeptic about philosophical
questions, and abandoned, almost to the point of heresy,
the rational arguments which were supposed to prove or
justify Christian theology. But with great psychological insight he showed how a Christian might regard all mundane
knowledge as in the last resort vain and as equally irrelevant
to his true spiritual needs.

Descartes was a loyal Catholic and at the same time a
systematic philosopher who found a place for the truths
of Christian theology and of mathematical physics in his
scheme. The necessity of God's existence had to be proved
before the certainty of any of our natural knowledge could
be guaranteed; and he accepted some of the traditional
proofs of the existence of God. The realm of extended things
is wholly separated from the realm of souls who think, and
the causes which operate in one realm have no directly deducible effects in the other. Human beings are composite
beings, and are the meeting point of the two realms; they
are partly minds which think, partly bodies which are
governed by the universal laws of physics. Descartes, unlike Spinoza, was not in his published works primarily concerned with moral problems; his interest was in natural
philosophy. And even in natural philosophy he was prepared not to publish the conclusions which he had reached
if they would be disagreeable to the Church. His whole
philosophy, however incoherent it might be as an account
of man's position in nature, seemed an acceptable com-
promise between the claims of mathematical physics and
the claims of Christian theology. It was immediately acceptable therefore as the advanced thought of the time, and
dominated its century until Locke's *Essay* was published.
Clear thought and rational argument were increasingly
identified with the Cartesian method of analyzing complex
ideas into their simple components and of deducing con-

sequences from the most simple, self-evident propositions, in the manner of pure mathematics.

The conditions of thought in England, following the Reformation, were largely different from France, and the seventeenth century was the age of French predominance both in thought and in manners. With the publication of Locke's *Essay* English thought, and specifically English empiricism, spread across the Channel and formed the basis of radical thought throughout Europe in the eighteenth century. Bacon at the beginning of the century was equally a European figure, a point of reference for every philosopher of the time, but he was rather the last philosopher of the Renaissance than the first philosopher of the seventeenth century. He did not allow for the all-important place of mathematics in the organization of natural knowledge. And the seventeenth century can properly be called, in the history of philosophy, the Age of Reason, because almost all the great philosophers of the period were trying to introduce the rigor of mathematical demonstration into all departments of knowledge, including philosophy itself. The form of philosophical argument in Descartes, Spinoza and Leibniz is largely deductive and a priori; their intention was to prove their conclusions about the ultimate constituents of reality, and the limits of human knowledge, as a mathematical theorem is proved. Hume and Kant have long ago convinced most philosophers, particularly English and American philosophers, that deductive metaphysics of this kind must be empty and without content, and that no conclusions about the ultimate nature of things can be established by purely a priori argument. And in the last thirty years the possibility of any systematic construction in philosophy has been called in question again, on the ground that philosophy must be concerned with the analysis of concepts and of the meanings of words, and not with assertions or denials of existence. Perhaps some change in the nature of scientific problems, or in the conception of physical theory, or in the study of language itself, will at some time re-create the need for systematic philosophy; there may come a time when, as in the seventeenth century, some speculative synthesis seems the only way of understanding new forms of knowledge and of making their relationships clear. In the meantime, Descartes, Leibniz and Spinoza are read, not only as formative figures in European thought, but also for the richness and variety of their analyses of the concepts upon which our thought depends—for their analyses of knowledge and certainty, appearance and reality, existence and identity, freedom and necessity, mind and matter, deduction and experiment. These, among others, are the continuing problems of philosophy which present themselves in new forms in every age; and the best way of approaching them is to see how they have presented themselves to the greatest thinkers of the past.

int, in one respect, typical of the discursive method in science. He was a subtle, many-sided, prolific writer, but implicated in the corrupt politics of modern. There is a magnificence and a directness in the writing of in his life. His mind was full of projects and various learning, and he had a sharp appetite for new creations and curiosity. His former essays show his shrewd and sophistication. But he had not the hard sense of science in the shade of my tradition, the line of speculation of one in the great philosophers.

CHAPTER I

Bacon

FRANCIS BACON WAS BORN IN LONDON IN 1561 INTO A family connected on both sides with the Court and government, and he was always destined for great offices. He studied law at Gray's Inn and sought office and promotion from his uncle, William Cecil. Failing to obtain from Cecil the advancement he wanted, he attached himself to the Earl of Essex, who, in 1593, nominated him as attorney general. But, after long hesitation, Queen Elizabeth refused to accept him for that post.

When Essex's armed rebellion failed, Bacon was one of his accusers. After the accession of James I, Bacon's advance to power began. In 1603 he was knighted; in 1606 he married a rich heiress, and in 1607 he was made solicitor general and in 1613 attorney general. As a friend of James's favorite, George Villiers, he became a privy councilor in 1616, lord keeper in 1617, and, finally, lord chancellor and Baron Verulam in 1617. In 1621 he was made Viscount St. Albans. But, falling from favor, he was accused of accepting bribes, deprived of all his offices, and, after a short imprisonment, he retired to the country. He died in 1626.

Bacon stands outside the circle of the great philosophers of the seventeenth century; in spirit and outlook he belongs rather to the sixteenth century than to the age of the new mathematical physics and of rationalism in philosophy. Unlike Descartes, he had no vision of the application of mathematics in the study of nature and he made no lasting contribution to the analysis of concepts or of the different categories of thought. But his great works, the *Novum Organum* (1620) and the *Advancement of Learning* (1605), had an immense influence throughout Europe and

his name became a symbol of the inductive method in
science. He was a subtle, many-sided, prolific thinker, half
medieval in his conceptions and half modern. There is a
magnificence and disorder in his writing as in his life. His
mind was full of projects and various learning, and he had
a sharp appetite for new sensations and curiosities. His
famous essays show his subtlety and sophistication. But he
had not the hard sense of relevance in abstract argument,
the love of logic, which we find in the great philosophers,
and, above all, in Descartes, Spinoza and Leibniz. His eye
was always caught by the color and variety of concrete
things in nature before he had followed an argument far
enough among generalities. In short, he had the temperament of a naturalist rather than a philosopher.

Bacon, like Descartes, proclaimed a new method in the
sciences; but his method, unlike Descartes's, was not to involve a priori reasoning to indubitable truths. He advocated a purely empirical, experimental method which, starting from observations of particular things and events, would
move towards wider and wider generalization. These general statements, unlike those of mathematics, would be
capable of being proved false by experiment. His interest
is thus primarily in an *inductive* method, by which one
arrives from observation of fact at generalizations which
are merely probable. It is as a contributor to "inductive
logic" and experimental method that he has a permanent
place in the history of philosophy. Hume and Mill were
to carry further the investigation which Bacon began. He
turns his attention to topics wider than the methods of
empirical observation, to the function of scientific generalization and the design of fruitful experiment. He is
concerned also with the "notions" used in empirical inquiries, and suggests that philosophers must analyze the
language of science. By gaining a clear idea of the concepts
employed, they would eradicate those confusions of language which hamper empirical investigations from the beginning. He has also a theory of classification, of the principles which should guide us in natural history and in
making an inventory of the natural objects around us. We
should not classify things simply on the basis of superficial

resemblances, but should turn our attention to those divisions of kind in nature which are the most far-reaching and systematic. It was such a fundamental method of classification that Linnaeus (1735) introduced into the science of botany, so providing new foundations for natural knowledge.

The following extracts include examples both of his criticisms of the scholastic logic of science and of his positive recommendations. He attacks Aristotelian logic from several points of view. First, being based on the syllogism, it concentrated attention on the valid deductions of particular statements from more general statements, and ignored the problem of how these general statements are reached. Secondly, he showed that the generalization from particulars, as it is represented in scholastic logic, is hasty and superficial (see Aphorisms 1, 19, 22, 25). Traditional logic is equally inadequate in its account of the formation of "notions" and classes (see Aphorism 14). Thirdly, it suffers from the more fundamental disadvantage of being merely a method of recording knowledge already obtained (Aphorism 12); it is not a method of discovery, suggesting further research, and it cannot lead either to practical control over nature (Aphorisms 3, 4, 8), or to the discovery of new sciences (Aphorism 5).

In the place of this concentration on the orderly arrangement of general statements and of their particular instances in the syllogism, Bacon suggests a method of discovering more and more new and true statements of fact. The method of induction by simple enumeration—that is the mere listing of what is seen to occur together in nature—is to be replaced by a method of systematic experiment, which will rely on "proper rejections and exclusions." Thus, to take a very simple example, if some conjunction of features $a, b, c,$ is observed, it is not enough merely to record it and to go on recording similar particular matters of fact indefinitely; one must make experiments which will leave out systematically each one of the features in turn, and so enable us to discover, for instance, that only a or only b is necessary for the production of $c,$ and not both a and b together; or, if they are found to be jointly necessary, to find some more general, common feature of them in virtue of which they are always followed by c. Here we see the need for the analysis and classification of notions which Bacon demands; for, if the scientist relies on a fund of common language which has some confused term serving as the name of a and b, taken together, he will not be able to separate them in his mind and so will never think of the experiment which is needed.

Perhaps Bacon's most profound observation was that the scientist must recognize the superior power of negative instances (Aphorism 46). If he has made a generalization of the form "whenever a happens b happens," he must always look for a case of a happening without b. If this negative instance is found, he must look for the most fruitful way of amending his law, and not be content with introducing some "frivolous distinction" (Aphorism 25). It is the essence of superstition to pay attention only to the positive instances which support one's beliefs and not to look for counter examples. Lastly, generalization must be as wide and embracing as is possible compatibly with the known facts and with the structure of existing science, and not merely wild, arbitrary or isolated (Aphorism 106). If we do not observe these principles, generalizations will be merely designed to fit the facts already known and will lead to no new discoveries. They are useless unless they have greater logical power than the particular statements on which they are based, that is, unless they imply that certain observations will be made outside the domain from which the generalization was derived. Here Bacon notices the truth that it is the broadness of its application that gives a scientific theory its power and usefulness.

Bacon's remarks on the logic of induction are tentative and often veiled in obscure terminology. But there are glimpses of that logic of experiment which was later fully expounded by John Stuart Mill. Bacon correctly stresses the importance of "putting nature to the question" systematically and in pursuit of a general hypothesis, rather than of merely recording observed facts on no constant principle. Perhaps he was too simply empirical, and his logic is still more easily applicable to the sciences of classi-

fication than to physics. He was inferior to Galileo and
Descartes in his vision of the future. He did not foresee the
physics of differential equations.

The extracts that follow are from the edition of James
Spedding; the first is from the Preface to the *Novum Organum*.

[Now my method, though hard to practise, is easy to
explain, and it is this. I propose to establish progressive
stages of certainty. The evidence of the sense, helped and
guarded by a certain process of correction, I retain. But
the mental operation which follows the act of sense I
for the most part reject; and instead of it I open and lay
out a new and certain path for the mind to proceed in,
starting directly from the simple sensuous perception.
The necessity of this was felt no doubt by those who
attributed so much importance to Logic, showing thereby that they were in search of helps for the understanding, and had no confidence in the native and spontaneous process of the mind. But this remedy comes too
late to do any good, when the mind is already, through
the daily intercourse and conversation of life, occupied
with unsound doctrines and beset on all sides by vain
imaginations. And therefore that art of Logic, coming (as I
said) too late to the rescue, and no way able to set matters right again, has had the effect of fixing errors rather
than disclosing truth. . . . There remains but one course for
the recovery of a sound and healthy condition,— namely,
that the entire work of the understanding be commenced
afresh, and the mind itself be from the very outset not left
to take its own course, but guided at every step; and the
business be done as if by machinery. Certainly if in things
mechanical men had set to work with their naked hands,
without help or force of instruments, just as in things intellectual they have set to work with little else than the
naked forces of the understanding, very small would the
matters have been which, even with their best efforts applied in conjunction, they could have attempted or accomplished. . . .]

The following is from the *First Book of Aphorisms*.

[III

Human knowledge and human power meet in one; for where the cause is not known the effect cannot be produced. Nature to be commanded must be obeyed; and that which in contemplation is as the cause is in operation as the rule.

IV

Towards the effecting of works, all that man can do is to put together or put asunder natural bodies. The rest is done by nature working within.

VII

The productions of the mind and hand seem very numerous in books and manufactures. But all this variety lies in an exquisite subtlety and derivations from a few things already known; not in the number of axioms.

VIII

Moreover the works already known are due to chance and experiment rather than to science; for the sciences we now possess are merely systems for the nice ordering and setting forth of things already invented; not methods of invention or directions for new works.

XI

As the sciences which we now have do not help us in finding out new works, so neither does the logic which we now have help us in finding out new sciences.

XII

The logic now in use serves rather to fix and give stability to the errors which have their foundation in commonly received notions than to help the search after truth. So it does more harm than good.

XIV

The syllogism consists of propositions, propositions consists of words, words are symbols of notions. Therefore if the notions themselves (which is the root of the matter) are confused and over-hastily abstracted from the facts, there can be no firmness in the superstructure. Our only hope therefore lies in a true induction.

XIX

There are and can be only two ways of searching into and discovering truth. The one flies from the senses and particulars to the most general axioms, and from these principles, the truth of which it takes for settled and immovable, proceeds to judgment and to the discovery of middle axioms. And this way is now in fashion. The other derives axioms from the senses and particulars, rising by a gradual and unbroken ascent, so that it arrives at the most general axioms last of all. This is the true way, but as yet untried.

XXII

Both ways set out from the senses and particulars, and rest in the highest generalities; but the difference between them is infinite. For the one just glances at experiment and particulars in passing, the other dwells duly and orderly among them. The one, again, begins at once by establishing certain abstract and useless generalities, the other rises by gradual steps to that which is prior and better known in the order of nature.

XXIV

It cannot be that axioms established by argumentation should avail for the discovery of new works; since the subtlety of nature is greater many times over than the subtlety of argument. But axioms duly and orderly formed from particulars easily discover the way to new particulars, and thus render sciences active.

XXV

The axioms now in use, having been suggested by a
scanty and manipular experience and a few particulars of
most general occurrence, are made for the most part just
large enough to fit and take these in: and therefore it is
no wonder if they do not lead to new particulars. And if
some opposite instance, not observed or not known before,
chance to come in the way, the axiom is rescued and preserved by some frivolous distinction; whereas the truer
course would be to correct the axiom itself.

XXXI

It is idle to expect any great advancement in science
from the superinducing and engrafting of new things upon
old. We must begin anew from the very foundations, unless
we would revolve for ever in a circle with mean and con-
temptible progress.

XXXVI

One method of delivery alone remains to us; which is
simply this: We must lead men to the particulars themselves, and their series and order; while men on their side
must force themselves for awhile to lay their notions by
and begin to familiarise themselves with facts.

XLVI

The human understanding when it has once adopted an
opinion (either as being the received opinion or as being
agreeable to itself) draws all things else to support and
agree with it. And though there be a greater number and
weight of instances to be found on the other side, yet
these it either neglects and despises, or else by some distinction sets aside and rejects; in order that by this great
and pernicious predetermination the authority of its former conclusions may remain inviolate. And therefore it
was a good answer that was made by one who when they
showed him hanging in a temple a picture of those who

had paid their vows as having escaped shipwreck, and
would have him say whether he did not now acknowledge
the power of the gods,—"Aye," asked he again, "but where
are they painted that were drowned, after their vows?"
And such is the way of all superstition, whether in astrology,
dreams, omens, divine judgments, or the like; wherein
men, having a delight in such vanities, mark the events
where they are fulfilled, but where they fail, though this
happen much oftener, neglect and pass them by. But with
far more subtlety does this mischief insinuate itself into
philosophy and the sciences; in which the first conclusion
colours and brings into conformity with itself all that come
after, though far sounder and better. Besides, independently of that delight and vanity which I have described, it
is the peculiar and perpetual error of human intellect to be
more moved and excited by affirmatives than by negatives;
whereas it ought properly to hold itself indifferently disposed towards both alike. Indeed in the establishment of
any true axiom, the negative instance is the more forcible
of the two.

C

But not only is a greater abundance of experiments to
be sought for and procured, and that too of a different kind
from those hitherto tried; an entirely different method, order, and process for carrying on and advancing experience
must also be introduced. For experience, when it wanders
in its own track, is, as I have already remarked, mere
groping in the dark, and confounds men rather than in-
structs them. But when it shall proceed in accordance with
a fixed law, in regular order, and without interruption, then
may better things be hoped of knowledge.

CIV

The understanding must not however be allowed to
jump and fly from particulars to remote axioms and of almost the highest generality (such as the first principles,
as they are called, of arts and things), and taking stand
upon them as truths that cannot be shaken, proceed to

prove and frame the middle axioms by reference to them; which has been the practice hitherto; the understanding being not only carried that way by a natural impulse, but also by the use of syllogistic demonstration trained and inured to it. But then, and then only, may we hope well of the sciences, when in a just scale of ascent, and by successive steps not interrupted or broken, we rise from particulars to lesser axioms; and then to middle axioms, one above the other; and last of all to the most general. For the lowest axioms differ but slightly from bare experience, while the highest and most general (which we now have) are notional and abstract and without solidity. But the middle are the true and solid and living axioms, on which depend the affairs and fortunes of men; and above them again, last of all, those which are indeed the most general; such I mean as are not abstract, but of which those intermediate axioms are really limitations.

The understanding must not therefore be supplied with wings, but rather hung with weights, to keep it from leaping and flying. Now this has never been done; when it is done, we may entertain better hopes of the sciences.

CV

In establishing axioms, another form of induction must be devised than has hitherto been employed; and it must be used for proving and discovering not first principles (as they are called) only, but also the lesser axioms, and the middle, and indeed all. For the induction which proceeds by simple enumeration is childish; its conclusions are precarious, and exposed to peril from a contradictory instance; and it generally decides on too small a number of facts, and on those only which are at hand. But the induction which is to be available for the discovery and demonstration of sciences and arts, must analyse nature by proper rejections and exclusions; and then, after a sufficient number of negatives, come to a conclusion on the affirmative instances; which has not yet been done or even attempted, save only by Plato, who does indeed employ this form of induction to a certain extent for the purpose of discussing definitions and ideas. But in order to furnish this induction or demon-

stration well and duly for its work, very many things are
to be provided which no mortal has yet thought of: insomuch that greater labour will have to be spent in it than
has hitherto been spent on the syllogism. And this induction
must be used not only to discover axioms, but also in the
formation of notions. And it is in this induction that our
chief hope lies.

CVI

But in establishing axioms by this kind of induction, we
must also examine and try whether the axiom so established be framed to the measure of those particulars only
from which it is derived, or whether it be larger and wider.
And if it be larger and wider, we must observe whether by
indicating to us new particulars it confirm that wideness
and largeness as by a collateral security; that we may not
either stick fast in things already known, or loosely grasp
at shadows and abstract forms; not at things solid and realised in matter. And when the process shall have come
into use, then at last shall we see the dawn of a solid hope.]

The following is Aphorism X from the *Second Book of
Aphorisms*.

[Now my directions for the interpretation of nature embrace two generic divisions; the one how to educe and
form axioms from experience; the other how to deduce
and derive new experiments from axioms. The former again
is divided into three ministrations; a ministration to the
sense, a ministration to the memory, and a ministration
to the mind or reason.

For first of all we must prepare a *Natural and Experimental History,* sufficient and good; and this is the foundation of all; for we are not to imagine or suppose, but to
discover, what nature does or may be made to do.

But natural and experimental history is so various and
diffuse, that it confounds and distracts the understanding,
unless it be ranged and presented to view in a suitable order. We must therefore form *Tables and Arrangements of*

Instances, in such a method and order that the understanding may be able to deal with them.

And even when this is done, still the understanding, if left to itself and its own spontaneous movements, is incompetent and unfit to form axioms, unless it be directed and guarded. Therefore in the third place we must use *Induction,* true and legitimate induction, which is the very key of interpretation.]

CHAPTER II

Galileo

GALILEO GALILEI (1564-1642), THE GREAT ASTRONOMER, was born at Pisa. He was both a brilliant experimental scientist and a mathematician, and became professor of mathematics at the University of Pisa. At the age of nineteen he had already observed the equality of oscillation of a simple pendulum; he later arrived at the proposition that all bodies, whatever their weight, descend with equal velocity. He proceeded to demonstrate his generalization experimentally, in spite of the fact that it removed the basis of the orthodox Aristotelian physics. He became famous throughout Europe, and, at Padua, and under the protection of the Medici family in Florence, he went on to make further revolutionary discoveries. Perhaps the greatest of them was the design for a refracting telescope. Using this telescope, he made a series of observations which seemed to him to confirm Copernicus's hypothesis that the sun is the center of the system of the heavens. He also arrived at the conclusion that the Milky Way is a vast path of separate stars. These deductions from observation were gradually to transform man's conception of his place in the universe and particularly his conception of the size of the universe in relation to man himself. The tidy Aristotelian universe, with man on earth as its physical, as well as its moral, center, was destroyed. We shall see how the great philosophers of the century, particularly Spinoza and Leibniz, tried to represent the immensities of the universe in their conceptual scheme.

The Catholic church condemned Galileo's discoveries as incompatible with doctrine, and ultimately attacked Galileo in person. When he was seventy years old and in bad health he was called before the Inquisition and, after a prolonged trial, compelled to disclaim his true opinions. He was reprieved by outside intervention from the dungeons of the Inquisition and retired to Florence to make further discoveries in physics. The Church had hoped to crush the statement of truth, based on observation of fact, by an exercise of power. It failed, with ignominy.

Galileo's magnificent achievements were based on two principles which have become the guiding principles of modern science: first, that in making statements and hypotheses about nature one must always appeal to observation and not to authority; secondly, that natural processes can best be understood if they are represented in mathematical terms. These principles are stated in his "Dialogue Concerning the Two Great Systems of the World."

The second of these principles is stated in the first of the two extracts from *Il Saggiatore* given below (Question 6): by "philosophy" is meant "natural philosophy," which includes the whole of science. The second extract (Question 48) states that physical nature is to be understood, and represented in science, solely in terms of its directly measurable properties, "shape, quantity and motion." This distinction between what came to be called Primary Qualities, which are the directly measurable qualities of things, and Secondary Qualities (odors, tastes, sounds, colors) runs all through the philosophy of the century following Galileo.

Secondary qualities are represented as in some way subjective and unreal, being mere ideas produced in us by the action of physical realities on our sense organs. Physical nature itself, apart from our perception of it, is exactly as it is described in the laws of physics and mechanics, and not as it is described in our ordinary language. It was left to Bishop Berkeley in the next century to question this assumption that the primary qualities can intelligibly be said to exist without secondary qualities. The distinction which Galileo is here making was assumed to be valid and necessary by Descartes and is the foundation of his philosophy of nature.

[Philosophy is written in that vast book which stands forever open before our eyes, I mean the universe; but it cannot be read until we have learnt the language and become familiar with the characters in which it is written. It is written in mathematical language, and the letters are triangles, circles and other geometrical figures, without which means it is humanly impossible to understand a single word.

No sooner do I form a conception of a material or corporeal substance, than I feel the need of conceiving that it has boundaries and shape: that relative to others it is great or small; that it is in this or that place and in this or that time; that it is moving or still; that it touches or does not touch another body; that it is one, few or many; nor can I, by any effort of imagination, dissociate it from these properties. On the other hand. I find no need to apprehend it as accompanied by such properties as to be white or red, bitter or sweet, sounding or silent, pleasant or evil smelling. Perhaps, if the senses had not informed us of these qualities, the reason and imagination alone would never have arrived at them. Therefore I hold that these tastes, odors, colors, etc., of the object in which they seem to reside, are nothing more than pure names, and exist only in the sensitive being; so that if the latter were removed these qualities would themselves vanish. But having given them special names different from those of the other primary and real qualities, we would persuade ourselves that they also exist just as truly and really as the latter. . . . But I hold that there exists nothing in external bodies for exciting in us tastes, odors and sounds but size, shape, quantity and slow or swift motion. And I conclude that if the ears, tongue and nose were removed, shape, quantity and motion would remain but there would be no odors, tastes or sounds, which apart from living creatures I believe to be mere words.]

CHAPTER III

Hobbes

THOMAS HOBBES WAS BORN IN 1588 AND DIED IN 1679. HE
was known for his remarkable memory and his wit. He
became a private tutor attached to the Cavendish family,
and traveled in France and Italy. He worked with Francis
Bacon, whom he did not respect as a philosopher, and he
was deeply impressed by the physics of Galileo, whom he
later visited in Italy. He became interested in optics, one
of the developing sciences of the time. He read Descartes
with great excitement. In 1640 he wrote *The Elements of
Law* as a defense of absolutism, but thought it necessary
to take refuge in France when he foresaw the coming tri-
umph of the parliamentarians. He remained there until
1651. The Latin adaptation of his work on law, published
in Paris under the title of *De Cive*, was put on the index
of prohibited books by the Church. In Paris he followed
English politics during the Revolution with passionate interest, and he had foreseen Cromwell's success. He wrote
his great work, the *Leviathan*, to recommend a powerful
secular state, whether republican or royalist, to act independently of the Church, and shocked the Stuart Court at
St. Germain, at which he had been living. In 1651 he returned to London, and even worked for Cromwell, while
remaining friendly with Royalists. In 1655 the first part
of his *De Corpore* was published, which again contained
attacks on the influence of priests. He had been tutor to
Charles II while in France, and welcomed him in London
at the Restoration. But his militant atheism was unpopular
and he could not republish his earlier works. He was still
writing at the age of ninety.

He was a man of strong personality, witty, sharp, brilliant, and of powerful physique; he admired strength, authority and lucidity of mind. He despised superstition and

feared the influence of sects and churches. He was a famous
figure of his age and a symbol of independence of mind,
often feared and execrated.

Hobbes was a materialist and skeptic, who attacked
scholastic philosophy as being a meaningless play with
meaningless words—"absurd speeches . . . without any
significance at all." Words have meaning only when they
are associated, directly or indirectly, with qualities of sense
or feeling. Qualities of sense or feeling are produced by the
motions of bodies acting on our body; these motions leave
traces, and associations are set up. This engenders memory
and imagination, which is "nothing but decaying sense."
But men have the capacity to attach names to their imaginations, and to use signs; and some names are universal
names, which stand for a "similitude in some quality."
"Truth consists in the right ordering of names in our affirmation," and we are apt to be "entangled in words" unless
we attend carefully to the definitions of words. Philosophers, unlike geometers, have written nonsense, because
they have not followed the geometrical method of beginning
with clear definitions; by this method the conclusions of
geometry have been made indispensable, and philosophy
should imitate it. Spinoza was later to follow in his *Ethics*
this suggestion that philosophical arguments should be set
out in geometrical form. Hobbes himself tries to base the
argument of the *Leviathan* on clear definitions; the reading
of Euclid's *Elements* was a determining influence in his
philosophy. He tried to build a philosophy of mind, and
to account for the workings of the mind, using solely the
facts of memory and imagination. Reasoning is mere calculation, the manipulation of signs, and the reasoning is
correct if the same signs are constantly attached to the
same images. The science of mechanics shows the pattern
which human reasoning should follow; for in mechanics
we calculate the movements of bodies according to the law
of cause and effect, and the movements of the human mind
can be calculated in the same way. From this mechanistic
philosophy of the human mind he deduced the simple
theory of sentiment and appetite, on which his political
philosophy was based.

His political philosophy was of greater originality and of more permanent importance than his theory of knowledge. But the following extracts illustrate, first, his rejection of scholastic abstractions and, secondly, his doctrine of words as signs, and of the necessity of clear definitions. In his attempt to prove, by appeal to clear definitions and scientific method, that traditional metaphysics was meaningless, he may be compared with the logical positivists of the twentieth century. He deliberately formed a style which was coarse, direct, unpedantic and shocking; he wanted to make the philosophy of the schools ridiculous, and to bring the argument down to brass tacks—the brass tacks of materialism and cool, common sense. His abrupt, mocking, eccentric personality can be felt in his paragraphs, very much as it is described by Aubrey in his *Brief Lives*.

The extracts that follow, from the first three chapters of the *Leviathan,* illustrate the tough materialist basis of Hobbes's philosophy of mind. He starts from a simple causal notion of perception, which pictures it as a transaction between external objects and the sense organs, which sets up a train of motion in the "brain and heart"; these motions, reverberating later, give rise to "imagination." Hobbes uses the term "imagination" for any experience of having mental images (as he himself calls them); and classifies memory merely as a particular way of speaking of imagination, when we wish to emphasize the past origin of the images.

In giving this account of perceptions, Hobbes is influenced almost entirely by what we should call physical or physiological considerations. He is not really alive, as Descartes was, to the *philosophical* questions that arise about perception, the problems of how we know what external objects are really like, whether they exist as we perceive them, questions which were later in the English tradition to be the main concern of Locke and Berkeley. But he does hold the then current doctrine that the only qualities that are really "in" objects are those of extension, shape, and motion: it is the "motions" in objects that produce in us a sensation of the other qualities of color, hardness, heat and so on, which we wrongly suppose to be qualities of the objects themselves. This doctrine was elaborated by Locke in his distinction between "primary" and "secondary" qualities; it was subjected to radical criticism by Berkeley, who argued that there could be no more reason for saying that the so-called primary qualities were "in" objects, independently of an observer, than for saying that the secondary qualities were.

Hobbes next turns to the "train of imagination," as he calls it. Here we find that Hobbes did not, as is sometimes said, suppose that all thinking is conducted in words; he clearly has in mind thinking by means of mental images. But it is hardly thinking in a distinctively rational sense. He discusses prediction and retrodiction, that is, inferences to the future and to the past, considering them (appropriately in the present context) in terms of *expectation,* a nonrational state of mind brought about by past experience and habit. Prudence, the ability to be right about the future, he considers merely as a matter of conditioning; and indeed remarks that animals can sometimes in this respect be superior to human beings.

[CHAPTER I. Of Sense

Concerning the thoughts of man, I will consider them first singly and afterwards in train, or dependence upon one another. Singly, they are every one a representation or appearance, of some quality, or other accident of a body without us; which is commonly called an object. Which object works on the eyes, ears and other parts of a man's body; and by diversity of working, produces diversity of appearances.

The original of them all is that which we call sense; (For there is no conception in a man's mind, which has not at first, totally, or by parts, been begotten upon the organs of sense.) The rest are derived from that original. . . .

The cause of sense, is the external body, or object, which presses the organ proper to each sense, either immediately, as in the taste and touch; or mediately, as in seeing, hearing, and smelling; which pressure, by the mediation of nerves, and other strings and membranes of the body, continued

inwards to the brain and heart, causes there a resistance, or
counter pressure, or endeavour of the heart, to deliver itself:
which endeavour because *outward*, seems to be some matter
without. And this *seeming*, or *fancy*, is that which men
call sense; and consists, as to the eye, in a *light*, or *colour
figured*; to the ear, in a *sound*; to the nostril, in an *odour*;
to the tongue and palate, in a *savour*; and to the rest of the
body, in *heat, cold, hardness, softness*, and such other qualities, as we discern by *feeling*. All which qualities called
sensible, are in the object which causes them, but so many
several motions of the matter, by which it presses our organs diversely. Neither in us that are pressed, are they any
thing else, but divers motions; (for motion produces nothing
but motion.) But their appearance to us is fancy, the same
waking, that dreaming. And as pressing, rubbing, or strik-
ing the eye, makes us fancy a light; and pressing the ear
produces a din; so do the bodies also that we see or hear
produce the same by their strong, though unobserved actions. For if those colours and sounds were in the bodies
or objects that cause them, they could not be severed from
them, as by glasses, and in echoes by reflection, we see they
are; where we know the thing we see is in one place; the
appearance in another. And though at some certain distance, the real, the very object seems invested with the
fancy it begets in us; yet still the object is one thing, the
image or fancy is another. So that sense in all cases, is
nothing else but original fancy, caused (as I have said)
by the pressure, that is, by the motion, of external things
upon our eyes, ears, and other organs thereunto ordained.

But the Philosophy schools through all the Universities
of Christendom, grounded upon certain texts of Aristotle,
teach another doctrine; and say, for the cause of *vision*
that the thing seen sendeth forth on every side a *visible
species* (in English) a *visible show, apparition*, or *aspect*,
or a *being seen*, the receiving of which into the eye is
seeing. And for the cause of *hearing*, that the thing heard
sends forth an *audible species*, that is an *audible aspect*, or
audible being seen; which entering at the ear, makes *hearing*. For the cause of *understanding* also, they say the thing
understood sends forth *intelligible species*, that is, an *intel-*

ligible being seen; which coming into the understanding, makes us understand. I do not say this as disapproving the use of Universities; but because I am to speak hereafter of their office in a Commonwealth I must let you see on all occasions by the way, what things would be amended in them; amongst which the frequency of insignificant speech is one.

CHAPTER II. Of Imagination

That when a thing lies still, unless something else stir it, it will lie still for ever, is a truth that no man doubts. But that when a thing is in motion it will eternally be in motion, unless something else stop it, though the reason be the same, (namely, that nothing can change itself,) is not so easily assented to. For men measure, not only other men, but all other things, by themselves: and because they find themselves subject after motion to pain, and lassitude, think every thing else grows weary of motion, and seeks repose of its own accord; little considering whether it may not be some other motion, in which that desire of rest they find in themselves consists. From hence it is that the Schools say, heavy bodies fall downward, out of an appetite to rest, and to conserve their nature in that place which is most proper to them: ascribing appetite and knowledge of what is good for their conservation, (which is more than man has,) to inanimate things, absurdly.

When a body is once in motion it moves (unless something else hinder it) eternally; and whatsoever hinders it, cannot in an instant, but in time, and by degrees, quite extinguish it: and as we see in the water, though the wind cease, the waves do not give over rolling for a long time after; so also it happens in that motion, which is made in the internal parts of a man, then, when he sees, dreams, etc. For after the object is removed, or the eye shut, we still retain an image of the thing seen, though more obscure than when we see it. And this is what the Latins call *Imagination*, from the image made in seeing; and apply the same, though improperly, to all the other senses. But the Greeks call it *Fancy*; which signifies *appearance*, and is as proper to one sense as to another IMAGINATION therefore is nothing but *decaying sense;* and is found in men, and many other living creatures, as well sleeping as waking.

The decay of sense in men waking, is not the decay of the motion made in sense; but an obscuring of it, in such manner, as the light of the sun obscures the light of the stars; which stars do no less exercise their virtue, by which they are visible, in the day, than in the night. But because amongst many strokes, which our eyes, ears, and other organs receive from external bodies, the predominant only is sensible; therefore the light of the sun being predominant, we are not affected with the action of the stars. And any object being removed from our eyes, though the impression it made in us remain; yet other objects more present succeeding. and working on us, the imagination of the past is obscured, and made weak; as the voice of a man is in the noise of the day. From which it follows that the longer the time is, after the sight. or sense of any object, the weaker is the imagination. For the continual change of man's body destroys in time the parts which in sense were moved: so that distance of time, and of place, has one and the same effect in us. For as at a great distance of place, that which we look at appears dim, and without distinction of the smaller parts; and as voices grow weak and inarticulate: so also after great distance of time, our imagination of the past is weak; and we lose (for example) of cities we have seen, many particular streets; and of actions, many particular circumstances. This *decaying sense,* when we would express the thing itself, (I mean *fancy* itself,) we call *Imagination,* as I said before: but when we would express the *decay,* and signify that the sense is fading, old, and past, it is called *Memory*. So that *Imagination* and *Memory* are but one thing, which for divers considerations has divers names.

Much memory, or memory of many things, is called *Experience*. Again, Imagination being only of those things which have been formerly perceived by Sense, either all at once, or by parts at several times; the former, (which is the imagining the whole object, as it was presented to the sense) is *simple Imagination;* as when one imagines a man, or horse, which he has seen before. The other is *compounded;* as when from the sight of a man at one time, and of a horse at another, we conceive in our mind a Centaur. So when a man compounds the image of his own person, with the image of the actions of another man; as when a man imagines himself a Hercules, or an Alexander, (which happens often to those who are much taken with reading of Romances) it is a compound imagination, and properly but a fiction of the mind. There are also other imaginations that rise in men, (though waking) from the great impression made in sense: as from gazing upon the sun, the impression leaves an image of the sun before our eyes a long time after; and from being long and vehemently intent upon geometrical figures, a man shall in the dark, (though awake) have the images of lines, and angles before his eyes: which kind of fancy has no particular name; as being a thing that does not commonly fall into men's discourse.

The imaginations of them that sleep, are those we call *Dreams.* And these also (as all other imaginations) have been before, either totally, or by parcels in the sense. And because in sense, the brain, and nerves, which are the necessary organs of sense, are so benumbed in sleep as not easily to be moved by the action of external objects, there can happen in sleep, no imagination; and therefore no dream, but what proceeds from the agitation of the inward parts of man's body; which inward parts, for the connection they have with the brain and other organs, when they are distempered, keep the same in motion; whereby the imaginations formerly made there appear as if a man were waking: saving that the organs of sense being now benumbed, so that there is no new object which can master and obscure them with a more vigorous impression, a dream must necessarily be more clear, in this silence of sense, than are our waking thoughts. And so it comes to pass that it is a hard matter, and by many thought impossible to distinguish exactly between sense and dreaming. For my part, when I consider that in dreams I do not often, nor constantly, think of the same persons, places, objects and actions that I do waking; nor remember so long a train of coherent thoughts, dreaming, as at other times; and because waking I often observe the absurdity of dreams, but never dream of the absurdity of my waking thoughts; I am well satisfied that, being awake, I know I dream not; though when I dream, I think myself awake. . . .

The imagination that is raised in man (or any other creature indued with the faculty of imagining) by words, or other voluntary signs, is what we generally call *Understanding;* and is common to man and beast. For a dog will understand by custom the call, or the rating of his master; and so will many other beasts. That understanding which is peculiar to man, is the understanding not only of his will; but his conceptions and thought, by the sequel and contexture of the names of things into affirmations, negations and other forms of speech. . . .

Chapter III. Of the Consequence or Train of Imaginations

By *Consequence,* or TRAIN of thoughts, I understand the succession of one thought to another, which is called (to distinguish it from discourse in words) *Mental Discourse.*

When a man thinks on anything whatsoever, his next thought after is not altogether so casual as it seems to be. Not every thought to every thought succeeds indifferently. But as we have no imagination, whereof we have not formerly had sense, in whole or in parts; so we have no transition from one imagination to another, whereof we never had the like before in our senses. The reason for which is this. All fancies are motions within us, relics of those made in the sense: and those motions that immediately succeeded one another in the sense, continue also together after sense: in so much as the former coming again to take place, and be predominant, the latter follows, by coherence of the matter moved, in such manner as water upon a plain table is drawn which way any one part of it is guided by the finger. But because in sense, to one and the same thing perceived, sometimes one thing, sometimes another succeeds, it comes to pass in time that in the imagining of any thing there is no certainty as to what we shall imagine next; only this is certain, it shall be something that succeeded the same before, at one time or another.

This train of thoughts, or mental discourse, is of two sorts. The first is *unguided, without design,* and inconstant; wherein there is no passionate thought, to govern and direct those that follow to itself, as the end and scope of some desire, or other passion: in which case the thoughts are said to wander, and seem impertinent one to another as in a dream. Such are commonly the thoughts of men that are not only without company, but also without care of anything; though even then their thoughts are as busy as at other times, but without harmony; as the sound which a lute out of tune would yield to any man; or in tune, to one who could not play. And yet in this wild ranging of the mind, a man may often perceive the way of it, and the dependance of one thought upon another. For in a discourse of our present civil war, what could seem more impertinent than to ask (as one did) what was the value of a Roman Penny? Yet the coherence to me was manifest enough. For the thought of the war introduced the thought of the delivering up the king to his enemies, the thought of that brought in the thought of the delivering up of Christ; and that again the thought of the 30 pence. which was the price of that treason: and from this easily followed that malicious question; and all this in a moment of time; for thought is quick.

The second is more constant; as being *regulated* by some desire, and design. For the impression made by such things as we desire, or fear, is strong and permanent, or, (if it cease for a time) of quick return: so strong it is sometimes as to hinder and break our sleep. From desire arises the thought of some means we have seen produce the like of that which we aim at; and from the thought of that, the thought of means to that mean; and so continually, till we come to some beginning within our own power. And because the end, by the greatness of the impression, comes often to mind, in case our thoughts begin to wander, they are quickly again reduced into the way: which observed by one of the seven wise men, made him give this precept, which is now worn out, *Respice finem;* that is to say, in all your actions, look often upon what you would have, as the thing that directs all your thoughts in the way to attain it. . . .

Sometimes a man desires to know the event of an action; and then he thinks of some like action past, and the events thereof one after another; supposing like events will follow like actions. As he that foresees what will become of a criminal, re-cons what he has seen follow on the like crime before; having this order of thoughts, the crime, the officer, the prison, the judge, and the gallows. Which kind of thoughts is called *Foresight,* and *Prudence,* or *Providence;* and sometimes *Wisdom;* though such conjecture, through the difficulty of observing all circumstances, is very fallacious. But this is certain; by how much one man has more experience of things past, than another; by so much also he is more prudent, and his expectations the seldomer fail him. The *Present* only has a being in Nature; things *Past* have a being in the memory only, but things *to come* have no being at all; the *Future* being but a fiction of the mind, applying the sequels of actions past to the actions that are present; which with most certainty is done by him that has most experience; but not with certainty enough. And though it be called prudence, when the event answers our expectation; yet in its own nature, it is but presumption. For the foresight of things to come, which is Providence, belongs only to him by whose will they are to come. From him only, and supernaturally, proceeds prophecy. The best prophet naturally is the best guesser; and the best guesser, he that is most versed and studied in the matters he guesses at: for he has most *signs* to guess by.

A *sign* is the event antecedent of the consequence; and contrarily, the consequence of the antecedent, when the like consequences have been observed before: and the oftener they have been observed, the less uncertain is the sign. And therefore he that has most experience in any kind of business, has most signs, whereby to guess at the future time; and consequently is the most prudent: and so much more prudent than he that is new in that kind of business, as not to be equalled by any advantage of natural and extemporary wit: though perhaps many young men think the contrary.

Nevertheless it is not prudence that distinguishes man from beast. There are beasts that, at a year old, observe more, and pursue that which is for their good, more prudently, than a child can do at ten.

As prudence is a *Presumption* of the *Future,* contracted from the *Experience* of time *Past*: so there is a presumption of things past taken from other things (not future but) past also. For he that has seen by what courses and degrees a flourishing State has first come into civil war, and then to ruin; upon the sight of the ruins of any other State, will guess, the like war and the like courses have been there also. But this conjecture has the same uncertainty almost as the conjecture of the Future; both being grounded only upon experience.

There is no other act of man's mind, that I can remember, naturally planted in him, so as to need no other thing, to the exercise of it, but to be born a man, and live with the use of his five senses. Those other faculties, of which I shall speak by and by, and which seem proper to man only, are acquired, and increased by study and industry; and of most men learned by instruction and discipline; and all proceed from the invention of words, and speech. For besides sense and thoughts, and the train of thoughts, the mind of man has no other motion; though by the help of speech, and method, the same faculties may be improved to such a height, as to distinguish men from all other living creatures.

Whatsoever we imagine, is *Finite*. Therefore there is no Idea, or conception of any thing we call *Infinite*. No man can have in his mind an Image of infinite magnitude; nor conceive infinite swiftness, infinite time, or infinite force, or infinite power. When we say any thing is infinite, we signify only that we are not able to conceive the ends, and bounds of the thing named; having no conception of the thing, but of our own inability. And therefore the Name of *God* is used, not to make us conceive him; (for he is *Incomprehensible;* and his greatness and power are unconceivable;) but that we may honour him. Also because whatsoever (as I said before,) we conceive, has been perceived first by sense, either all at once, or by parts; a man

can have no thought, representing any thing, not subject to
sense. No man therefore can conceive any thing, but he
must conceive it in some place; and imbued with some
determinate magnitude; and which may be divided into
parts; nor that any thing is all in this place, and all in another place at the same time; nor that two, or more things
can be in one and the same place at once: for none of these
things ever have, or can be, incident to sense; but are absurd speeches, taken upon credit (without any significance
at all,) from deceived Philosophers, and deceived, or de-
ceiving, School men.]

THE DISTINCTION BETWEEN MEN AND ANIMALS LIES, FOR
Hobbes, in the possession of language; what he has to say
about language will be seen in his second group of extracts.

About language, and the uses of it, Hobbes has many
extremely interesting and valuable ideas; and he was re-
markably sensitive to the philosophical dangers of falling
into nonsense. His accusations of this failing are liberally
and somewhat hastily distributed; but the unfairness and
superficiality of many of his criticisms, and the sketchiness
of his own doctrines, are compensated by his great shrewd-
ness and originality, and by the unfailing verve and humor
with which he lays about him.

The "marks" or "notes" that make up language, when
they are used as names of things, he calls "signs." Signs can
be the names of objects, either of single objects (proper
names), or of many (common names). Not all names, however, refer directly to things in nature; there are also the
names of names, terms which (in the modern phrase) "refer intra-linguistically." Hobbes thinks that the assumption
that all words—e.g. abstract nouns—refer to some independently existent entities is a fruitful source of philosophical
errors; there is general agreement on this today, and the
sorts of consideration which he sketches have been widely
developed and refined by analytic philosophers in the last
thirty years. He also rightly observes that language is not
always used to make statements, but also, for instance, to
express our intentions and emotions. In his idea that we
use language about God not to describe, but to honor Him,

we see a brilliant foreshadowing of the theories of emotive, and of other nondescriptive, uses of language which are constantly under discussion among philosophers now.

About the old philosophical question of how common, or general, terms get their meaning—the so-called problem of universals—Hobbes is intransigently radical. The problem turned in part on the questions "What have all the things that fall under a general term in common?" or "What binds the indefinitely large class of such things together?"; and to this Hobbes answers: "Nothing, except the possession of the common name which we attach to them." This position of extreme nominalism, like any other simple answer to such an involved question, is an exaggeration, but many would now agree that it was at least an exaggeration in the right direction. Hobbes gives no consideration to the difficulties involved, and dismisses the various theories which supposed that there must be some common property to hold the class together.

The possession of language enables man's thinking to take the form, not just of a train of mental images, but of a reckoning of "the consequences of terms." Hobbes regards these as two different ways of thinking about *things*: with his usual common sense, he says that words stand directly for things, and not, as Locke and his successors later misleadingly insisted, for ideas. He seems to consider that the advantage of verbal thinking over image thinking lies in the greater generality given by the use of general terms; he gives the example of a man without knowledge of language who, he claims, could *in a particular case* "see" that the angles of a triangle were equal to two right angles from mere inspection of the figures. How the man's success in this feat is to be accomplished, or to be recognized by others, Hobbes does not explain; nor does he explain how this is to be reconciled with what he elsewhere says, that all deductions consist in the working out of the "consequences of terms." In general he rightly regards the necessary truth of a deductive inference as lying in the logical interrelations of the meanings of the terms employed.

When he comes to consider the statements of science, Hobbes's usual empiricism deserts him. For he thinks *all*

scientific thinking is just the following out of the "consequences of terms," and that any statement made must be
true, if it is true at all, in virtue of the meanings of the
terms employed in it. Truth, he says, consists in "the right
ordering of names in our affirmations"; and falsehood consequently must be the same as absurdity in the application
and use of terms. In modern terms, Hobbes regards all true
statements as "analytic," and all false ones as self-contradictory. All science, then, will be like a geometrical deductive system: that is, on Hobbes's own view, it will be
a linguistic calculus and the validity of the inferences in it
will be guaranteed by the definitions adopted. But such a
system could not possibly, by itself, give us an empirical
science: for no provision is made for observations of what
actually happens, or for predictions of future events.

In his view of science, the rationalist model of geometry
as the ideal form of knowledge—"the only Science that it
has pleased God hitherto to bestow on mankind"—has over-
ridden the natural tendency of his thought. Had he merely
re-expressed, in terms of prediction and hypothesis, what
he had already said about prudence and "presumption of
the future," he could have given a more accurate account
of the falsifiable inductive conclusions with which science
works.

The last extract from Hobbes, which comes from the
fourth book of the *Leviathan,* is highly characteristic of
him. In attacking the theory of separate essences, which he
inaccurately attributes to Aristotle, he makes the valuable
observation that one must not base philosophical theories
merely on the grammatical forms of one's own language,
and suggests that there could easily be a language which had
no equivalent of "is" to provide the copula in such predi-
cations as "a man is a living body." (He got this idea, it
seems, from some knowledge about Chinese.) This is a
valuable philosophical remark, even though it is combined
with the inadequate theory that all predication consists in
joining together two names of the same thing. Certainly
there is no such quick way with metaphysical theories, and
Hobbes has no time to linger over the arguments. The reasons for his haste emerge in the last paragraph of this

extract. Hobbes was not primarily concerned with the
problems of metaphysics and theory of knowledge at all.
His interest was in political theory, and in the philosophical
foundations of strong government; everything else is inci-
dental. Yet in considering these incidentals he shows very
great insight and power of mind; for all his crudities, he
was an original genius who contributed much to the rise of
British empiricism and who has been, in this respect, unduly
neglected. He has also a claim, which these extracts can
only inadequately illustrate, to be considered the most
amusing philosopher of his time. His scathing humor en-
livens the *Leviathan* from end to end.

[CHAPTER IV. Of Speech

. . . .

The general use of speech is to transfer our mental discourse into verbal; or the train of our thoughts into a train
of words; and that for two commodities; whereof one is
the registering of the consequences of our thoughts; which
being apt to slip out of our memory, and put us to a new
labour, may again be recalled, by such words as they were
marked by. So that the first use of names, is to serve for
Marks, or *Notes* of remembrance. Another is, when many
use the same words to signify (by their connection and
order) one to another, what they conceive, or think of each
matter; and also what they desire, fear, or have any other
passion for. And for this use they are called *Signs*. Special
uses of speech are these; first, to register, what by cogita-
tion, we find to be the cause of anything present or past;
and what we find things present or past may produce, or
effect: which in sum, is acquiring of Arts. Secondly, to
show to others that knowledge which we have attained;
which is, to counsel and teach one another. Thirdly, to
make known to others our wills and purposes, that we may
have the mutual help of one another. Fourthly, to please
and delight ourselves and others, by playing with our
words, for pleasure or ornament, innocently.

To these uses, there are also four correspondent abuses.
First, when men register their thoughts wrong, by the in-

constancy of the signification of their words; by which they register for their conceptions, that which they never conceived; and so deceive themselves. Secondly, when they use words metaphorically; that is, in other sense than that they are ordained for; and thereby deceive others. Thirdly, when by words they declare that to be their will which is not. Fourthly, when they use them to grieve one another: for seeing nature has armed living creatures, some with teeth, some with horns, and some with hands to grieve an enemy, it is but an abuse of speech to grieve him with the tongue, unless it be one whom we are obliged to govern; and then it is not to grieve, but to correct and amend.

The manner how speech serves to the remembrance of the consequence of causes and effects, consists in the imposing of *Names,* and the *Connection* of them. Of names, some are *Proper,* and singular to one thing only; as *Peter, John, this man, this tree*: and some are *Common* to many things: as *Man, Horse, Tree;* each of which though but one Name, is nevertheless the name of divers particular things; in respect of all which together, it is called a *Universal;* there being nothing in the world universal but names; for the things named are every one of them individual and singular.

One universal name is imposed on many things, for their similitude in some quality, or other accident: and whereas a Proper Name brings to mind one thing only, universals recall any one of those many.

And of universal names, some are of more, and some of less extent; the larger comprehending the less large; and some again of equal extent, comprehending each other reciprocally. As for example, the name *Body* is of larger signification than the word *Man,* and comprehends it; and the names *Man* and *Rational* are of equal extent, comprehending one another mutually. But here we must take notice, that by a name is not always understood, as in Grammar, one word only; but sometimes by circumlocution many words together. For all these words, *He that in his actions observes the Laws of his Country,* makes but one name, equivalent to this one word, *Just.*

By this imposition of names, some of larger, some of stricter signification, we turn the reckoning of the consequences of things imagined in the mind, into a reckoning of the consequences of appellations. For example, a man that has no use of speech at all, (such, as is born and remains perfectly deaf and dumb) if he set before his eyes a triangle, and by it two right angles, (such as are the corners of a square figure) he may by meditation compare and find, that the three angles of a triangle, are equal to those two right angles that stand by it. But if another triangle be shown him different in shape from the former, he cannot know without a new labour, whether the three angles of that also be equal to the same. But he that has the use of words, when he observes that such equality was consequent, not to the length of the sides, nor to any other particular thing in his triangle; but only to this, that the sides were straight, and the angles three; and that that was all, for which he named it a Triangle; will boldly conclude universally, that such equality of angles is in all triangles whatsoever; and register his invention in these general terms, *Every triangle has its three angles equal to two right angles*. And thus the consequence found in one particular, comes to be registered and remembered as a universal rule; and discharges our mental reckoning, of time and place; and delivers us from all labour of the mind, saving the first; and makes that which was found true *here*, and *now*, to be true in *all times and places*.

.   .   .   .

When two names are joined together into a consequence, or affirmation; as thus, *A man is a living creature;* or thus, *if he be a man, he is a living creature,* if the latter name *living creature,* signify all that the former name *Man* signifies, then the affirmation, or consequence is *true;* otherwise *false*. For *True* and *False* are attributes of speech, not of things. And where speech is not, there is neither *Truth* nor *Falsehood. Error* there may be, as when we expect that which shall not be; or suspect what has not been: but in neither case can a man be charged with Untruth.

Seeing then that *Truth* consists in the right ordering of names in our affirmations, a man that seeks precise *truth,*

needs to remember what every name he uses stands for;
and to place it accordingly; or else he will find himself
entangled in words, as a bird in lime-twigs; the more he
struggles, the more belimed. And therefore in Geometry,
(which is the only Science that it has pleased God hitherto
to bestow on mankind) men begin at settling the signification of their words; which settling of significations they
call *Definitions;* and place them in the beginning of their
reckoning.

By this it appears how necessary it is for any man that
aspires to true Knowledge, to examine the definitions of
former authors; and either to correct them, where they are
negligently set down; or to make them himself. For the
errors of definitions multiply themselves, according as the
reckoning proceeds; and lead men into absurdities, which
at last they see, but cannot avoid, without reckoning anew
from the beginning; in which lies the foundation of their
errors. From whence it happens, that they that trust to
their books do as they that cast up many little sums into a
greater, without considering whether those little sums were
rightly cast up or not; and at last finding the error visible,
and not mistrusting their first grounds, do not know which
way to clear themselves; but spend time in fluttering over
their books; as birds that entering by the chimney, and
finding themselves enclosed in a chamber, flutter at the false
light of a glass window, for want of wit to consider which
way they came in. So that in the right definition of names,
lies the first use of speech; which is the acquisition of
science; and in wrong, or no definition, lies the first abuse;
from which proceed all false and senseless tenets; which
make those men that take their instruction from the authority of books, and not from their own meditation, to be
as much below the condition of ignorant men, as men
endued with true Science are above it. For between true
science, and erroneous doctrines, ignorance is in the middle.
Natural sense and imagination are not subject to absurdity.
Nature itself cannot err: and as men abound in copiousness
of language; so they become more wise, or more mad than
ordinary. Nor is it possible without Letters for any man
to become either excellently wise, or (unless his memory

be hurt by disease, or ill constitution of organs) excellently foolish. For words are wise men's counters, they do but reckon by them; but they are the money of fools, that value them by the authority of an Aristotle, a Cicero, or a Thomas, or any other Doctor whatsoever, if but a man.

* * * * * * * * * * * *

Chapter V. Of Reason, and Science

* * * * * * * * *

When a man reckons without the use of words, which may be done in particular things, (as when upon the sight of any one thing, we conjecture what was likely to have preceded, or is likely to follow upon it;) if that which he thought likely to follow, follows not; or that which he thought likely to have preceded it, has not preceded it, this is called ERROR; to which even the most prudent men are subject. But when we reason in words of general significa- tion, and fall upon a general inference which is false; though it be commonly called *Error*, it is indeed an ABSURDITY, or senseless speech. For error is but a deception, in pre- suming that something is past, or to come; of which, though it were not past, or not to come; yet there was no impos- sibility discoverable. But when we make a general asser- tion, unless it be a true one, the possibility of it is uncon- ceivable. And words whereby we conceive nothing but the sound, are those we call *Absurd, Insignificant,* and *Non- sense* And therefore if a man should talk to me of a *round Quadrangle;* or *accidents of Bread in Cheese;* or *imma- terial Substances;* or *a free Subject; a free-Will;* or any *Free,* but free from being hindered by opposition, I should not say he were in an Error; but that his words were with- out meaning; that is to say, absurd.

I have said before, (in the second chapter) that a Man excelled all other animals in this faculty, that when he conceived any thing whatsoever, he was apt to enquire the consequences of it, and what effects he could do with it. And now I add this other degree of the same excellence, that he can by words reduce the consequences he finds to general rules, called *Theoremes,* or *Aphorisms;* that is, he can reason, or reckon, not only in number; but in all other things, in which one may be added to, or subtracted from another.

But this privilege is allayed by another; and that is by the privilege of absurdity; to which no living creature is subject, but man only. And of men, those are of all most subject to it that profess Philosophy. For it is most true that *Cicero* says of them somewhere; that there can be nothing so absurd, but may be found in the books of Philosophers. And the reason is manifest. For there is not one of them that begins his ratiocination from the definitions, or explications of the names they are to use; which is a method that has been used only in Geometry; whose conclusions have thereby been made indisputable.

The first cause of absurd conclusions I ascribe to the want of method; in that they do not begin their ratiocination from definitions; that is, from settled significations of their words: as if they could cast account, without knowing the value of the numerical words, *one, two,* and *three.*

And whereas all bodies enter into account upon divers considerations, (which I have mentioned in the precedent chapter;) these considerations being diversely named, divers absurdities proceed from the confusion, and unfit connection of their names into assertions. And therefore

The second cause of absurd assertions, I ascribe to the giving of names of *bodies, to accidents;* or of *accidents* to *bodies;* as they do that say, *Faith is infused,* or *inspired;* when nothing can be *poured,* or *breathed* into any thing, but body; and that, *extension is body;* that *phantoms* are *spirits,* etc.

The third I ascribe to the giving of the names of the *accidents* of *bodies without us,* to the *accidents* of our own *bodies;* as they do that say, the *colour is in the body; the sound is in the air,* etc.

The fourth, to the giving of the names of *bodies,* to *names,* or *speeches;* as they do that say, that *there be things universal;* that *a living creature is Genus,* or *a general thing,* etc.

The fifth, to the giving of the names of *accidents,* to *names* and *speeches;* as they do that say, *the nature of a thing is its definition; a man's command is his will;* and the like.

The sixth, to the use of Metaphors, Tropes, and other rhetorical figures, instead of words proper. For though it be lawful to say (for example) in common speech, *the way goes, or leads hither, or thither, The Proverb says this or that* (whereas ways cannot go, nor Proverbs speak) yet in reckoning, and seeking of truth, such speeches are not to be admitted.

The seventh, to names that signify nothing; but are taken up, and learned by rote from the Schools, as *hypostatical, transubstantiate, consubstantiate, eternal-Now,* and the like canting of School men.

To him that can avoid these things, it is not easy to fall into any absurdity, unless it be by the length of an account; in which he may perhaps forget what went before. For all men by nature reason alike, and well, when they have good principles. For who is so stupid, as both to mistake in Geometry, and also to persist in it, when another detects his error to him?   .   .   .   .]

The following is from Chapter 46, "Of the darkness from vain philosophy and fabulous traditions," *Leviathan,* Part IV, "The Kingdom of Darkness."

[Now to descend to the particular tenets of vain philosophy derived to the Universities, and thence into the church, partly from Aristotle, partly from blindness of understanding; I shall first consider their principles. There is a certain *Philosophia Prima,* on which all other philosophy ought to depend; and consisteth principally, in right limiting of the significations of such appellations, or names, as are of all others the most universal: which limitations serve to avoid ambiguity, and equivocation in reasoning; and are commonly called definitions; such as are the definitions of body, time, place, matter, form, essence, subject, substance, accident, power, act, finite, infinite, quantity, quality, motion, action, passion, and divers others, necessary to the explaining of a man's conceptions concerning the nature and generation of bodies. The explication (that is, the settling of the meaning) of which, and the like terms, is commonly in the Schools called *Metaphysics;* as being a part of the philosophy of Aristotle, which hath that for title; but it is in another sense for there it signifieth as much, as *Books written, or placed after his natural philosophy*: But the Schools take them for *Books of supernatural philosophy*: for the word *metaphysics* will bear both these senses. And indeed that which is there written, is for the most part so far repugnant to natural reason, that whosoever thinketh that there is anything to be understood by it, must needs think it supernatural.

From these metaphysics, which are mingled with the scripture to make School divinity, we are told, there be in the world certain essences separated from bodies, which they call *abstract essences, and substantial forms*: for the interpreting of which *jargon*, there is need of somewhat more than ordinary attention in this place Also I ask pardon of those who are not used to this kind of discourse, for applying myself to those that are. The world (I mean not the earth only, that denominates the lovers of it *worldly men,* but the *universe* that is, the whole mass of all things that are) is corporeal, that is to say, body; and hath the dimensions of magnitude, namely, length, breadth, and depth: also every part of body, is likewise body, and hath the like dimensions; and consequently every part of the universe, is body; and that which is not body, is not part of the universe: and because the universe is all, that which is not part of it, is *nothing;* and consequently *no where.* Nor does it follow from hence, that spirits are *nothing;* for they have dimensions, and are therefore really *bodies;* though that name in common speech be given to such bodies only, as are visible, or palpable; that is, that have some degree of opacity: but for spirits, they call them incorporeal; which is a name of more honour, and may therefore with more piety be attributed to God himself; in whom we consider not what attribute expresseth best his nature, which is incomprehensible; but what best expresseth our desire to honour him.

To know now upon what grounds they say there be

essences abstract, or *substantial forms,* we are to consider what those words do properly signify. The use of words is to register to ourselves, and make manifest to others, the thoughts and conceptions of our minds. Of which words, some are the names of the things conceived; as the names of all sorts of bodies, that work upon the senses, and leave an impression in the imagination: others are the names of the imaginations themselves; that is to say, of those ideals, or mental images we have of all things we see, or remember: and others again are names of names; or of different sorts of speech: as *universal, plural, singular,* are the names of names; and *definition, affirmation, negation, true, false, syllogism, interrogation, promise, covenant,* are the names of certain forms of speech. Others serve to show the consequence, or repugnance of one name to another; as when one saith, *a man is a body,* he intendeth that the name of *body* is necessarily consequent to the name of *man;* as being but several names of the same thing, *man;* which consequence is signified by coupling them together with the word *is.* And as we use the verb *is;* so the Latins use their verb *est,* and the Greeks their ἐστι, through all its declinations. Whether all other nations of the world have in their several languages a word that answereth to it, or not, I cannot tell; but I am sure they have not need of it; for the placing of two names in order may serve to signify their consequence, if it were the custom, (for custom is it, that gives words their force) as well as the words *is,* or *be,* or *are,* and the like.

And if it were so, that there were a language without any verb answerable to *est,* or *is,* or *be;* yet the men who used it would be not a jot the less capable of inferring, concluding, and of all kind of reasoning, than were the Greeks, and Latins. But what then would become of these terms, of *entity, essence, essential, essentiality,* that are derived from it, and of many more that depend on these, applied as most commonly they are? They are therefore no names of things; but signs, by which we make known, that we conceive the consequence of one name or attribute to another: as when we say, *a man, is, a living body,* we mean not that the *man* is one thing, the *living body* another, and the *is,* or *being*

a third; but that the *man,* and the *living body,* is the same
thing; because the consequence, *if he be a man, he is a
living body,* is a true consequence, signified by that word
Is. Therefore, *to be a body, to walk, to be speaking, to live,
to see,* and like infinitives; also *corporeity, walking, life,
sight,* and the like that signify just the same, are the names
of *nothing;* as I have elsewhere more amply expressed.

But to what purpose (may some man say) is such sub-
tility in a work of this nature, where I pretend to nothing
but what is necessary to the doctrine of government and
obedience? It is to this purpose, that men may no longer
suffer themselves to be abused, by them, that by this doctrine of *separated essences,* built on the vain philosophy of
Aristotle, would fright them from obeying the laws of their
country, with empty names; as men fright birds from the
corn with an empty doublet, a hat, and a crooked stick. For
it is upon this ground, that when a man is dead and buried,
they say his soul (that is his life) can walk separated from
his body, and is seen by night amongst the graves. Upon
the same ground they say, that the figure, and colour, and
taste of a piece of bread, has a being, there, where they say
there is no bread: and upon the same ground they say, that
faith, and wisdom, and other virtues are sometimes *poured*
into a man, sometimes *blown* into him from Heaven; as if
the virtuous, and their virtues could be asunder; and a great
many other things that serve to lessen the dependence of
subjects on the sovereign power of their country. For who
will endeavour to obey the laws, if he expect obedience to be
poured or blown into him? Or who will not obey a priest,
that can make God, rather than his sovereign; nay than
God himself? Or who, that is in fear of ghosts, will not
bear great respect to those that can make the holy water,
that drives them from him? And this shall suffice for an
example of the errors, which are brought into the church,
from the *entities,* and *essences* of Aristotle; which it may
be he knew to be false philosophy; but writ it as a thing
consonant to, and corroborative of their religion; and fear-
ing the fate of Socrates.   .   .   .   .   .   .]

CHAPTER IV

Descartes

RENÉ DESCARTES WAS BORN IN 1596. HIS MOTHER DIED A year later, and he was brought up in the country by a tutor. He was educated by the Jesuits at La Flèche, and he was later to praise their teaching in the *Discourse on Method*. He studied law at Poitiers, but decided to travel and to study by himself in Paris. He was particularly interested in music and in fencing and he even wrote treatises on these subjects. He joined, as a volunteer, a force under Maurice of Nassau, which was fighting on the Protestant side in the Thirty Years' War; Descartes was always a loyal Catholic, but it was not unusual at the time for gentlemen to become soldiers of fortune, even though they were indifferent to the cause which they were defending in that confused war. Descartes's motive simply was to travel and to have leisure to think. While at Breda in Holland he decided to write a general treatise on mathematics and the mathematical sciences. While serving in Germany in 1620, he experienced at least two moments of illumination, or visions, in which his philosophy, or some parts of it, seemed to be revealed to him. In 1624 he went from France to Italy to render thanks for his visions to the Virgin Mary at Loretto. In 1629 he settled in Holland, determined to protect his privacy and independence. In 1637 the *Discourse on Method* was published at Leyden, and he was immediately recognized as the foremost philosopher of his age. He left Holland for Stockholm in 1649 at the invitation of Queen Christina, partly because he was increasingly involved in religious controversy in Holland; throughout his life he had tried to avoid polemics. He died of pneumonia in Stockholm in 1650.

He had published his *Meditations on the First Philosophy* in Paris in 1641, *Principia Philosophiae* in Amsterdam in 1644, the *Passions of the Soul* in Paris in 1649. A number of works, including the *Regulae Ad Directionem Ingenii* and *Traité du Monde,* remained to be published after his death.

Descartes is the type of the philosopher who avoids any entanglements or attachments, particularly in politics and public affairs. He was a solitary and entirely original thinker who had moments of pure inspiration, and the power to express his visions later with exquisite clarity. He was fascinated by mathematics and corresponded with Fermat, the great mathematician of his time. He had an extraordinary pride of intellect, and a visionary confidence in his own powers of mind. He did not acknowledge the necessity of a conflict between religion and modern science, and he thought that he had found the true adjustment between them in his philosophy. Withdrawn and quiet by temperament, he became one of the great revolutionaries of European thought by the compelling clarity and the subtle simplicity of his thought and language.

Mathematics is for Descartes the model of clear and certain knowledge, which advances step by step from one indisputable conclusion to another. Outside mathematics all claims to knowledge seem, when one pauses to reflect, uncertain, unsystematic, and unsupported by any common method of proof. The first step therefore is to introduce into the chaos of philosophy and physical science the clear and uniform deductive method of mathematics; only by system and method can knowledge be built upon sure foundations. The proper order in philosophy is to start from the most simple and clear truths, containing only the most simple notions, and to advance step by step towards more complex truths, making sure that each step of the argument is indisputable. In restarting philosophy from the beginning, one must reject every statement which can possibly be doubted, until one arrives at simple and self-evident truths which cannot possibly be doubted. These are the sure foundations of knowledge.

Descartes shows his method in action in the *Discourse* and *Meditations*, applying his method of doubt until he arrives at the indubitable proposition "I think, therefore I am." He also shows that he cannot doubt the existence of God. Using these two indubitable truths, he proceeds to show that we have reason to believe in the existence of the external world, although our ordinary judgments of perception are in themselves fallible and our senses may deceive us. When we have proved the existence of God, we have reason to trust that account of the world of spatial beings, called by Descartes Extension, which alone commends itself to our reason. Descartes distinguishes ideas in the mind from the external reality which, in the process of perception, imprints ideas on the mind. He then distinguishes the different kinds or types of idea in the mind. Only ideas which are entirely clear and distinct can be accepted into the structure of knowledge. And only the ideas which represent the true nature of external things, as this nature is made intelligible in mathematical physics, can be accepted as genuine knowledge.

The following extracts show only Descartes's method of criticizing claims to knowledge, his method of doubt, and his standard of certainty; for it is this critical investigation, rather than his constructive metaphysics, that has been permanently important. He may be called the founder of the modern theory of knowledge, since he made the questions "How do I know?" and "Can I be certain?" the first questions of philosophy. He was to be followed by the English empiricists in the next century, and by Bertrand Russell and others in this century, in looking for the foundations of knowledge in some propositions which are certain and indubitable. But he had also a positive philosophy of mind and a positive philosophy of physics. He conceived the realm of mind as wholly distinct from the realm of extended things; and he expressed this distinction in the traditional terms of substance and cause, with their medieval connotations. He believed also that there were certain ideas that are innate in the mind, and in no manner derived from experience. All these doctrines had presented them-

selves to him as parts of a single system, together with the
conception of human personality as an immaterial substance, the mind, lodged in a mechanical system, the body.
He was convinced that all the problems of science, mathematics and practical life are soluble by "the natural light"
of reason, following its own natural order. This unlimited
claim for "the natural light," and for the clear style and
method of thought which went with it, became the foundation of French civilization up till the French revolution.
The Encyclopedists and radicals of the next century were
his direct heirs in style and method, in spite of their difference of aim. He taught men to reject scholastic obscurities
and to think for themselves, confident that whatever seems
self-evident in the clear light of reason must be true. And
he invented a style which for nearly two centuries remained
the natural vehicle of French thought.

In the following passages of the *Discourse on Method*
(1637) Descartes explains how, by using the method of
systematic doubt, he arrives at the foundations of his system: knowledge of his own existence and of the existence
of God. His demonstration of his own existence as one un-
shakable fact, immune from the process of doubt, is of an
extreme and elegant simplicity. We are often deceived by
our senses, or suppose something to be true which is not
true, and obviously we do not know, at such moments, that
we are being deceived. Thus it is possible at *any* moment
to suppose that we are being deceived, for instance, that
we are dreaming, and we can sensibly doubt the genuine
existence of what seems to exist around us in the world.
But one thing we cannot doubt is that we are doubting; for
if we were to doubt that, we should still, once more, be
doubting. The self, Descartes argues, must be immune
from the doubt, for the self always re-enters with any doubt
that one has—it is always the self that doubts. But doubting is only a sort of thinking, and it is in virtue of its power
to think that the self is seen to exist. Hence Descartes's
fundamental proposition, *cogito ergo sum,* "I think, there-
for I am."

Descartes next asks what it is about this proposition

that makes it so certainly true, and finds the answer in the "clarity and distinctness" with which it appears to be true. This does not mean, as it might at first seem, that Descartes will just be satisfied with any proposition that seems, psychologically, to be obviously true. No philosophy could go very deep which did not examine critically many beliefs which, from unreflective habit, we do in fact feel to be certainly true. What Descartes is looking for as the foundations of his system are propositions which it is not just difficult to doubt, but nonsensical or contradictory to doubt. To think that one was not thinking (and thus to doubt the existence of one's own mind) seems to be, in a peculiar way, self-contradictory. Other propositions have this peculiar kind of self-evidence, and are such that it would be nonsensical to doubt their truth. In particular, there are the propositions of mathematics, which Descartes constantly takes as his model of how thought should proceed.

Descartes mentions various features of these indubitable propositions which help to explain what he means by their "clarity and distinctness." Their truth, unlike that of propositions about the external world, is independent of the conditions in which they are conceived: "If a geometer should conceive some new demonstration (when dreaming), the circumstance of his being asleep would not militate against its truth"; whereas if he had some empirical belief, for instance that he was flying or seeing the stars, it might well be false. Hence Descartes emphasizes that it is only on the evidence of our *reason,* and not on that of our imagination or senses, that we ought to be persuaded of the truth of anything. His fundamental thought is that the truth of an indubitable proposition must be *intrinsic* to it, not dependent on any external circumstances.

A proposition of the required kind must be, to use the scholastic term, a statement of *essence.* The essence of a thing, roughly, consists of those features of it which it must have, if it is to be that thing at all. Many features of a thing can be "thought away" without self-contradiction—it would be possible, for instance, for a table to have some color different from that which in fact it has—but there are some

characteristics which that thing must have if it is to be a
table at all, and these are its essential characteristics. The
second extract from Galileo in Chapter II shows him applying this idea, in a special way, to the notion of a material
body in physics; he names those qualities which it seems to
him are of the essence of such a body, without which it
cannot be conceived at all.

The statement of the essence of something fits admirably
the Cartesian requirements for a necessarily true proposition; it contains intrinsically the marks of its own truth,
ar.d we cannot conceive that the opposite should be true.
Thus Descartes, having arrived at the statement *"cogito
ergo sum,"* is able to say that the essence of his personal
identity, his "selfhood," must lie in his mind. He could
conceive of himself as not having a body, but not as not
having a mind; therefore the existence of his mind is seen
as what is essential to his existence as a person, while the
existence of his body, on the other hand, is "accidental,"
not essentially connected in this way with his existence.

This notion of essence Descartes applies also in the second step of the construction of his system, his proof of the
existence of God. For just as he found that in the idea of
a triangle is contained "the equality of its three angles to
two right angles"—this is part of its essence—so he found,
or claimed to find, that in the idea of a Perfect Being is
contained the idea of existence. Although he could make
various statements about the essence of a triangle, none
of them was to the effect that there in fact existed such a
thing as a triangle; but in the case of a Perfect Being, its
"existence is included in its essence"—one has only to gain
a clear idea of what a Perfect Being is, to see that such a
Being must exist.

This argument—which is similar to the famous "ontological proof" of the existence of God, invented by An-
selm—is only one of Descartes's proofs of this conclusion.
Starting, again, from the concept he in fact has of a Perfect
Being, he reasons that such an idea could not have arisen
merely from himself: for he himself is imperfect (as is
shown, for instance, by the fact that he doubts, a state of

mind inferior to pure knowledge), and it is evidently contrary to reason that the less perfect should give rise to the more perfect. Thus he claims to see contained in his own imperfection, and in that of anything else that may exist, a state of dependence on a Perfect Being; such a Being must therefore exist. This argument is highly characteristic of Descartes's position in the history of philosophy; it is very similar in form and terminology to a famed scholastic proof of the existence of God, the argument *"ex contingentia mundi,"* yet it is based, in a typically Cartesian way, on what is evident to the light of natural reason, to anyone who reflects on his own internal experience.

Having thus proved the existence of God, Descartes finds himself in a position to reconstruct those things the existence and truth of which he had previously doubted. For, he argues, the Perfect Being, whom we now know to exist, could not allow us to be completely and systematically deceived in the way we had supposed, and hence some reliance — with due allowance for the imperfection of any human observer — can be placed on the existence of those things that we normally suppose to be in the world about us. The nature of the things, and the laws that govern their behavior, can be discovered by application of those analytical and mathematical methods which, at the metaphysical level, Descartes has already been using. He admits elsewhere in the *Discourse* that not all can be done by pure a priori reasoning; the limitations of the human mind are such that experiments will be necessary to show the way. Ideally, however, an organized science will know the essence of each thing and so be able to deduce from that knowledge the whole body of mathematical laws that will explain the world.

In considering the foundations of Descartes's system, one is bound to ask what kind of peculiar self-evident necessity *does* characterize the propositions he establishes; and when we ask this, his reliance on the self-evident is seen to be less satisfactory than it seems at first. It is agreed that more is required than a mere psychological obviousness; reliance on this, as has been seen, could only lead to the perpetuation of error. The alternative, then, is a *logical* necessity; a proposition will in this sense be necessarily true if its opposite is self-contradictory. Yet if this is Descartes's sense, his fundamental conclusions are not of the right type. His whole system is based on propositions that assert *existence* — of his own mind, and of God. But philosophers since Kant are generally agreed that no proposition that asserts existence in this way can be logically necessary; and this now seems obvious. The logical relations of our language do not determine the contents of the universe.

Both Descartes's fundamental premises can be seen on closer inspection not to have the necessity he claims for them. The proposition "I am thinking," if necessary, should have an opposite which is self-contradictory; but "I am not thinking," which is its opposite, is not self-contradictory. Certainly, if anyone thinks it, it is false, but it is not self-contradictory, as is, for instance, "I am a married bachelor." We might, for example, imagine a man under an anaesthetic who made various remarks, and if one of these remarks were "I am not thinking," we could say that in that case it was true. A proper self-contradiction, however uttered or produced, must always be necessarily false. "I am thinking" is a proposition which can carry with it, in the circumstances of its consideration, the facts that make it true. There are other propositions of the same kind: such as "I am writing," when written, or "I am saying something in English," when spoken. "I am thinking" is one of the most general cases of this phenomenon.

Descartes is not justified in drawing from this proposition the more far-reaching conclusions of the kind he embraces, concerning the individual, substantial, noncorporeal and eternal nature of the mind that is doing the thinking. In the sense in which "I am thinking" is made true by thinking it, the "I" can have none of this content — it is a mere mark of reference. Alternatively, if "I" is supposed to have some content, and to contain the notions of individual personal existence, then the most that Descartes can properly conclude is *"cogitatur,"* "there is some thinking going on." Kant, in the *Critique of Pure Reason,* showed, with the greatest care and subtlety, how the whole pro-

gram of "rational psychology"–the Cartesian attempt to
pass from necessarily true premises to informative and substantial conclusions about the self–must be invalid.

Kant was also responsible for the final demolition of the
"ontological proof" of the existence of God. That argument depended on the idea that the existence of a Perfect
Being must be included in his essence, that it must be a
necessary property of such a being that he should exist.
But how could existence be connected by logical necessity
with a set of properties, however perfect? Existence, Kant
showed, is not a property, like largeness or redness—
rather a thing must exist before it can have any properties
at all.

It now seems that Descartes, in his search for a certainty
on which to base science, had turned his attention in the
wrong direction. He was fascinated by the necessary truths
of mathematics, and erected the mathematical kind of certainty into the canon for all statements that were to be
considered reputable. But certainty of this kind, by itself,
is insufficient for an empirical science; it lies in the purely
logical interrelations of a theory and can carry in itself no
predictive power or connection with the facts of experience.
Nor should empirical statements, because they lack this
certainty, be despised in comparison. Rather they can
have their own kind of "certainty." The possibility that
they may be proved false by later experience is not a disadvantage that they labor under, compared with the statements of mathematics, but rather the secret of their power.
Only thus can they serve to distinguish one empirical state
of affairs from another, and so assist us in understanding
nature, and putting its processes to our use. Descartes, in
common with other metaphysicians, had in mind the form
which a completed science would assume; he gave a picture
of what ideal knowledge would be, rather than of the actual
methods of science, subject to the actual limitations of
human knowledge.

[. . . I had long before noticed that, for the habits of ordinary life, it is sometimes necessary to adopt, as if above
doubt, opinions which we discern to be highly uncertain, as

has been already said; but as I then wanted to give my attention solely to the search after truth, I thought that a procedure exactly the opposite was called for, and that I ought to reject as absolutely false all opinions in regard to which I could suppose the least ground for doubt, in order to ascertain whether after that there remained anything in my belief that was wholly indubitable. Accordingly, seeing that our senses sometimes deceive us, I was willing to suppose that there existed nothing really such as they lead us to imagine; and because some men err in reasoning, and fall into paralogisms, even on the simplest matters of geometry, I, convinced that I was as open to error as any other, rejected as false all the reasonings that I had so far taken for demonstrations; and finally, when I considered that the very same thoughts which we have when awake may also come when we are asleep, while there is at that time not one of them true, I supposed that all the objects that had ever entered into my mind when awake, had in them no more truth than the illusions of my dreams. But immediately afterwards I observed that, whilst I thus wished to think that all was false, it was absolutely necessary that I, who thus thought, should be something; and as I observed that this truth, I think, therefore I am, was so certain and of such evidence, that no ground of doubt, however extravagant, could be alleged by the sceptics capable of shaking it, I concluded that I might, without scruple, accept it as the first principle of the philosophy of which I was in search.

In the next place, I attentively examined what I was and as I observed that I could suppose that I had no body, and that there was no world nor any place in which I might be; but that I could not therefore suppose that I was not; and that, on the contrary, from the very circumstance that I thought to doubt of the truth of other things, it most clearly and certainly followed that I was; while, on the other hand, if I had only ceased to think, although all the other objects which I had ever imagined had been in reality existent, I would have had no reason to believe that I existed; I thence concluded that I was a substance whose whole essence or nature consists only in thinking, and which, that it may exist, has need of no place, nor is dependent on any material thing; so that "I," that is to say, the mind by which I am what I am, is wholly distinct from the body, and is even more easily known than the latter, and is such, that although the latter were not, it would still continue to be all that it is.

After this I inquired in general into what is essential to the truth and certainty of a proposition; for since I had discovered one which I knew to be true, I thought that I must likewise be able to discover the ground of this certainty. And as I observed that in the words I think, therefore I am, there is nothing at all which gives me assurance of their truth beyond this, that I see very clearly that in order to think it is necessary to exist, I concluded that I might take, as a general rule, the principle, that all the things which we very clearly and distinctly conceive are true, only observing, however, that there is some difficulty in rightly determining the objects which we distinctly conceive.

In the next place, from reflecting on the circumstance that I doubted, and that consequently my being was not wholly perfect (for I clearly saw that it was a greater perfection to know than to doubt), I was led to inquire whence I had learned to think of something more perfect than myself; and I clearly recognised that I must hold this notion from some nature which in reality was more perfect. As for the thoughts of many other objects external to me, as of the sky, the earth, light, heat, and a thousand more, I was less at a loss to know whence these came; for since I remarked in them nothing which seemed to render them superior to myself, I could believe that, if these were true, they were dependencies on my own nature, in so far as it possessed a certain perfection, and, if they were false, that I held them from nothing, that is to say, that they were in me because of a certain imperfection of my nature. But this could not be the case with the idea of a nature more perfect than myself; for to receive it from nothing was a thing manifestly impossible; and, because it is not less

repugnant that the more perfect should be an effect of,
and dependent on, the less perfect, than that something
should proceed from nothing, it was equally impossible that
I could hold it from myself: accordingly, it only remained
that it had been placed in me by a nature which was in
reality more perfect than mine, and which even possessed
within itself all the perfections of which I could form any
idea; that is to say, in a single word, which was God. And
to this I added that, since I knew some perfections which
I did not possess, I was not the only being in existence (I
will here, with your permission, freely use the terms of the
Schools); but, on the contrary, that there was of necessity
some other more perfect Being upon which I was dependent, and from whom I had received all that I possessed; for if I had existed alone, and independently of
every other being, so as to have had from myself all the
perfection, however little, which I actually possessed, I
should have been able, for the same reason, to have had
from myself the whole remainder of perfection, of the
want of which I was conscious, and thus could of myself
have become infinite, eternal, immutable, omniscient, all-
powerful, and, in short, have possessed all the perfections
which I could recognise in God. For in order to know
the nature of God (following the arguments just mentioned), as far as my own nature permitted, I had only
to consider in respect of all the properties of which I found
in my mind some idea, whether their possession was a
mark of perfection; and I was assured that no one which
indicated any imperfection was in him, and that none of
the rest was wanting. Thus I perceived that doubt, incon-
stancy, sadness, and such like, could not be found in God,
since I myself would have been happy to be free from
them. Besides, I had ideas of many sensible and corporeal
things; for although I might suppose that I was dreaming,
and that all which I saw or imagined was false, I could
not, nevertheless, deny that the ideas were in reality in my
thoughts. But, because I had already very clearly recognised in myself that the intelligent nature is distinct from
the corporeal, and as I observed that all composition is

an evidence of dependence, and that a state of dependence is manifestly a state of imperfection, I therefore determined that it could not be a perfection in God to be compounded of these two natures, and that consequently he was not so compounded; but that if there were any bodies in the world, or even any intelligences, or other natures that were not wholly perfect, their existence depended on his power in such a way that they could not subsist without him for a single moment.

I was disposed straightway to search for other truths; and when I had represented to myself the object of the geometers, which I conceived to be a continuous body, or a space indefinitely extended in length, breadth, and height or depth, divisible into various parts which admit of different figures and sizes, and of being moved or transposed in all manner of ways (for all this the geometers suppose to be in the object they consider), I went over some of their simplest demonstrations. And, in the first place, I observed, that the great certainty which by common consent is accorded to these demonstrations, is founded solely upon this, that they are clearly conceived in accordance with the rule I have already laid down. In the next place, I perceived that there was nothing at all in these demonstrations which could assure me of the existence of their object: thus, for example, supposing a triangle to be given, I distinctly perceived that its three angles were necessarily equal to two right angles, but I did not on that account perceive anything which could assure me that any triangle existed: while, on the contrary, recurring to the examination of the idea of a Perfect Being, I found that the existence of the Being was contained in the idea in the same way that the equality of its three angles to two right angles is contained in the idea of a triangle, or as in the idea of a sphere, the equidistance of all points on its surface from the centre, or even still more clearly; and that consequently it is at least as certain that God, who is this Perfect Being, is, or exists, as any demonstration of geometry can be.

.   .   .   .

Finally, if there be still persons who are not sufficiently persuaded of the existence of God and of the soul, by the

reasons I have adduced, I very much wish that they should
know that all the other propositions, of the truth of which
they deem themselves perhaps more assured, as that we
have a body, and that there exist stars and an earth, and
such like, are less certain; for, although we have a moral
assurance of these things, which is so strong that there is
an appearance of extravagance in doubting their existence,
yet at the same time no one, unless he takes leave of reason, can deny, when the question relates to a metaphysical
certitude, that there is sufficient reason to exclude entire
assurance, in the observation that when asleep we can in
the same way imagine ourselves possessed of another body
and that we see other stars and another earth, when there
is nothing of the kind. For how do we know that the
thoughts which occur in dreaming are false rather than
those other which we experience when awake, since the
former are often not less vivid and distinct than the latter?
And though men of the highest genius study this question
as long as they please, I do not believe that they will be
able to give any reason which can be sufficient to remove
this doubt, unless they presuppose the existence of God.
For, in the first place, even the principle which I have already taken as a rule, viz., that all the things which we
clearly and distinctly conceive are true, is certain only
because God is or exists and because he is a Perfect Being,
and because all that we possess is derived from him:
whence it follows that our ideas or notions, which to the
extent of their clearness and distinctness are real, and
proceed from God, must to that extent be true. Accordingly, whereas we often enough have ideas or notions in
which some falsity is contained, this can only be the case
with such as are to some extent confused and obscure,
and in this have some share of nullity, that is, exist in us
thus confused because we are not wholly perfect. And
it is evident that it is not less repugnant that falsity or imperfection, in so far as it is imperfection, should proceed
from God, than that truth or perfection should proceed
from nothing. But if we did not know that all which is in
us of real and true proceeds from a Perfect and Infinite
Being, however clear and distinct our ideas might be, we

should have no ground on that account for the reassurance that they possessed the perfection of being true.

But after the knowledge of God and of the soul has made us certain of this rule, we can easily understand that the truth of the thoughts we have when awake, ought not in the slightest degree to be called in question on account of the imaginations of our dreams. For if it happened that an individual, even when asleep, had some very distinct idea, as, for example, if a geometer should discover some new demonstration, the circumstance of his being asleep would not militate against its truth; and as for the most ordinary error of our dreams, which consists in their representing to us various objects in the same way as our external senses, this is not significant as giving us an occasion to suspect the truth of the ideas of sense; for we are not infrequently deceived in the same manner when awake; as when persons who have jaundice see all objects yellow, or when the stars or bodies at a great distance appear to us much smaller than they are. For, in short, whether awake or asleep, we ought never to allow ourselves to be persuaded of the truth of anything unless on the evidence of our reason. And it must be noted that I say of our reason, and not of our imagination or of our senses: so, for example, although we very clearly see the sun, we ought not therefore to determine that it is only of the size which our sense of sight presents; and we may very distinctly imagine the head of a lion joined to the body of a goat, without being therefore driven to the conclusion that a chimaera exists; for it is not a dictate of reason that what we thus see or imagine is in reality existent; but it plainly tells us that all our ideas or notions must have some foundation in truth; for otherwise it could not be that God, who is wholly perfect and veracious, should have placed them in us. And because our arguments are never so clear or so complete during sleep as when we are awake, although sometimes the acts of our imagination are then as lively and distinct, if not more so, than in our waking moments, reason further dictates that, since all our thoughts cannot be true because of our partial imperfection, those possessing truth must infallibly be found in the experience of our waking moments rather than in that of our dreams.

. . . .

. . . But as soon as I had acquired some general notions in physics, and beginning to test them in various particular difficulties, had observed how far they can carry us, and how much they differ from the principles that have been employed up to the present time, I believed that I could not keep them concealed without offending gravely against the law by which we are bound to promote, as far as in us lies, the general good of mankind. For by them I perceived it to be possible to arrive at knowledge highly useful in life; and instead of the speculative philosophy usually taught in the schools, to discover a practical philosophy, by means of which, knowing the force and action of fire, water, air, the stars, the heavens, and all the other bodies that surround us, as distinctly as we know the various crafts of our artisans, we might also apply them in the same way to all the uses to which they are adapted, and thus make ourselves the lords and possessors of nature. . . .]

THE PREVIOUS EXTRACT GAVE ONLY THE BARE BONES OF Descartes's system; in the passages that follow, which are taken from *Meditations on the First Philosophy, in which the Existence of God and the Distinction between Mind and Body are demonstrated* (1641), we can gain a greater insight into some of its features. Here he gives at greater length his views on the absolute distinction between mind and body, the latter subject to mechanical causal laws, the former free from them and existing independently. This absolute distinction is of the first importance to Descartes's purpose of showing that the doctrines of the Catholic faith are reconcilable with progress and discovery in the physical sciences; the doctrines of religion are concerned with the soul, a substance quite separate from the processes of the physical world. He elaborates, also, his proofs of the existence of God, and says more of the method of doubt— a doubt which, it is worth noting, he considers as purely philosophical: in the synopsis, referring to the proofs of the external world which he offers in the sixth meditation, he remarks that he does not deem them "of great utility in establishing what they prove, viz., that there is in reality a world, that men are possessed of bodies, and the like, the truth of which no-one of sound mind ever seriously doubted." His point in giving such proofs is to show that they are less clear and certain than the demonstrations of the existence of mind and of God.

About the method of doubt Descartes makes here two principal new points. In the first meditation, he faces the difficulty that he claims to have proved the existence of a Perfect Being who could not allow us to be deceived, and yet it is a fact that we can be and sometimes are deceived, and Descartes's method has been to work on the assumption that we are. But why should a God who could not allow us always to be deceived allow us to be deceived sometimes? Faced with the problem of justifying the continued use of a method, the conclusion of which is that the method itself is unnecessary and perhaps blasphemous, Descartes invokes the idea of a malignant demon who, for the purposes of the method, may be supposed to be doing his best to mislead men into falsehood. A more serious answer to the problem is found in the fourth meditation, where he argues that it is a wrong use of man's free will that leads him into error: that by arrogantly making up his mind to a judgment where there are insufficient reasons to support it, he brings falsehood upon himself. For error, as for moral wickedness, God is not responsible. By the first suggestion, the blame was on the devil; by this, it is on man. Only by setting ourselves to accept nothing but what is by the Cartesian criterion genuinely acceptable, will we avoid error. This connection of belief and will, and the notion of what one can *choose to believe,* is of particular importance in the views of Pascal, who argued (very differently from Descartes) that there could be no necessary and compulsive demonstration of the existence of God; for, if there was, failure to believe in him would be evidence merely of stupidity, a failure of the understanding, whereas to be an unbeliever must constitute a failure of the will, a moral and not merely an intellectual error.

In the third meditation Descartes adds importantly to

those things that I cannot doubt. The original demonstration of something indubitable was in terms of thinking: the proposition "I am doubting." Here Descartes shows that the same considerations apply to the "imagination"; if I have an idea (by which he seems to mean a mental image), then at least I am certain *that I have such an idea,* even if the thing of which it is an idea does not in fact exist. The same is true of hallucinations — even if what I seem to see is not there, at least something is indubitably true, viz., that I seem to see it. This notion, that whatever else may be uncertain, the facts of my own experience cannot be uncertain, has figured again and again in the history of philosophy, down to the present day.

Descartes makes several approaches in these passages to the problem of the nature and existence of material objects. He is careful to distinguish "the power of the imagination" from "the power of the intellect": that is, the ability to imagine what a thing looks like from the knowledge of what in fact it is, of its nature. Here again he employs the notion of "essence," both in connection with the faculty of imagination, which, unlike that of intellectual thought, he considers to be an inessential feature of the mind; and in connection with the nature of external bodies. In the second meditation he seeks to prove that the essence of a piece of wax, for instance, cannot lie in its sensible qualities; for its sensible qualities can all change, as when we melt it, without our denying that it is the same piece of wax. Here Descartes relies on the importance and recurrent connection of essence with *identity*—the essence of a body, what it really is, is that which persists through change. From the independence of the essence of the wax from its sensible qualities, Descartes argues that knowledge of the nature of things is gained only by the intellect and not by the senses; and here we have one of his fundamental reasons for supposing that science, as the investigation of essences, is something which ideally should be independent of observation.

For the *existence* of material objects Descartes comes back in the end to his former argument from the nature of God. Among "ideas" he distinguishes what he calls

innate, factitious, and adventitious ideas — that is, those
that are already in the mind, those that are constructed by
the mind, and those that seem to arise spontaneously in
the mind whether we want them to or not. In the occurrence of the last he finds a sufficient reason for our *believing* that there exist objects external to us. That this
belief is correct can be established only by considerations
of the unwillingness of a Perfect Being to deceive us. There
is no intrinsic necessity in the existence of material objects.

In the fourth meditation Descartes goes so far as to
invoke the belief in God as the only ultimate safeguard
against error even in the case of propositions that are
clearly and distinctly conceived to be true. While such
propositions are indeed self-evident, when properly viewed,
it is possible to lose confidence in them through a lack of
attention, a mass of conflicting evidence, and other such
contingent factors; and since we can perhaps never be certain that we are not in such circumstances, it is only the
belief in the undeceiving God that preserves one's balance.
Here piety seems to have got the better of consistency. For
it will be remembered that the existence of such a God was
itself only proved by reflection on "clear and distinct ideas";
and so at this point Descartes does seem to have fallen
into the vicious circle of which he has often been accused.

Despite all the criticisms that can be brought against
him, Descartes is one of the still living philosophers. His
was a truly philosophical enterprise: the attention he gave
to the fundamental problems of our thought and knowledge helped to bring about a revolution in ideas, and many
of his questions are still with us. He stands in a uniquely
important position, with one foot in the scholastic past
and one in the science of the future. The theory of knowledge, in its modern form, begins with him.

[*Synopsis of the Six Following Meditations*

In the First Meditation I put forward the grounds on
which we may doubt in general of all things, and especially
of material objects, so long, at least, as we have no other
foundations for the sciences than those we have had up to
now. Now, although the utility of a doubt so general may

not be apparent at first sight, it is nevertheless of the greatest utility, since it delivers us from all prejudice, and affords the easiest pathway by which the mind may detach itself from the senses; and, finally, it makes it impossible for us to doubt wherever we afterwards discover truth.

In the Second, the mind which, in exercise of the freedom peculiar to itself, supposes that no object exists, of the existence of which it has even the slightest doubt, finds that, meanwhile, it must itself exist. And this point is also of the highest moment, for the mind is thus enabled easily to distinguish what belongs to itself, that is, to the intellectual nature, from what belongs to the body. But since some, perhaps, will expect, at this state of our progress, a statement of the reasons which establish the doctrine of the immortality of the soul, I think it proper now to warn them that it was my aim to write nothing of which I could not give exact proof, and that I therefore felt myself obliged to adopt an order similar to that in use among the geometers, viz., to set down everything upon which the proposition in question depends, before coming to any conclusion respecting it. Now, the first and chief prerequisite for the knowledge of the immortality of the soul is our being able to form the clearest possible conception of the soul itself, and such as shall be absolutely distinct from all our notions of body; and this is what is done in the passage in question. There is required, besides this, the assurance that all things which we clearly and distinctly conceive are true, exactly as we conceive them: and this could not be established before the Fourth Meditation. Further, it is necessary, for the same purpose, that we possess a distinct conception of corporeal nature, which is given partly in the Second and partly in the Fifth and Sixth Meditations. And, finally, on these grounds, we must conclude that all those objects which are *clearly and distinctly conceived to be diverse substances,* as mind and body, are substances really reciprocally distinct; and this inference is made in the Sixth Meditation. The absolute distinction of mind and body is, besides, confirmed in the Second Meditation, by showing that we cannot conceive body unless as divisible; while, on the other hand, mind cannot be conceived unless as indivisible. For we are not able to conceive the half of a mind, as we can of any body, however small, so that the natures of these two substances are to be held, not only as diverse, but even in some measure as contraries. I have not, however, pursued this discussion further in the present treatise, both for the reason that these considerations are sufficient to show that the destruction of the mind does not follow from the corruption of the body, and thus to afford men the hope of a future life, and also because the premises from which one can infer the immortality of the soul involve an explanation of the whole of physics: in order to establish, in the first place, that generally all substances, that is, all things which can exist only in consequence of having been created by God, are in their own nature incorruptible, and can never cease to be, unless God himself, by refusing his concurrence to them, reduce them to nothing; and, in the second place that body, taken generally, is a substance, and therefore can never perish, but that the human body, in as far as it differs from other bodies, is constituted only by a certain configuration of members, and by other accidents of this sort, while the human mind is not made up of accidents, but is a pure substance. For although all the accidents of the mind be changed — although, for example, it think certain things, will others, and perceive others — the mind itself does not vary with these changes; while, on the contrary, the human body is no longer the same if a change take place in the form of any of its parts: from which it follows that the body may, indeed, without difficulty perish, but that the mind is in its own nature immortal.

In the Third Meditation, I have explained at sufficient length, as appears to me, my chief argument for the existence of God. But yet, since I wished there to avoid the use of comparisons taken from material objects, that I might withdraw, as far as possible, the minds of my readers from the senses, numerous obscurities perhaps remain, which will, I trust, be afterwards entirely removed in the replies to the objections: thus, among other things, it may be difficult to understand how the idea of a being absolutely perfect, which is found in our minds, possesses so much objective reality [i.e., participates by representation in so many degrees of being and perfection] that it must be held to arise from a cause absolutely perfect. This is illustrated in the replies by the comparison of a highly perfect machine, the idea of which exists in the mind of some workman; for as the objective [i.e., representative] perfection of this idea must have some cause, viz., either the science of the workman, or of some other person from whom he has received the idea, in the same way the idea of God, which is found in us, demands God himself for its cause.

In the Fourth, it is shown that all which we very clearly and distinctly conceive is true; and, at the same time, is explained wherein consists the nature of error; points that require to be known as well for confirming the preceding truths, as for the better understanding of those that are to follow. But, meanwhile, it must be observed that I do not at all there treat of Sin, that is, of error committed in the pursuit of good and evil, but of that sort alone which arises in the determination of the true and the false. Nor do I refer to matters of faith, or to the conduct of life, but only to what regards speculative truths, and such as are known by means of the natural light alone.

In the Fifth, besides the illustration of corporeal nature, taken generally, a new proof is given of the existence of God, not free, perhaps, any more than the former, from certain difficulties, but of these the solution will be found in the replies to the objections. I further show in what sense it is true that the certainty of geometrical demonstrations themselves is dependent on the knowledge of God.

Finally, in the Sixth, the working of the understanding is distinguished from that of the imagination; the marks of this distinction are described; the human mind is shown to be really distinct from the body, and, nevertheless, to be so closely conjoined therewith as together to form something like a unity. All the errors which arise from the senses are brought under review, while the means of avoiding them are pointed out; and, finally, all the grounds are adduced from which the existence of material objects may be inferred; not, however, because I thought them very useful in establishing what they prove, viz., that there is in reality a world, that men are possessed of bodies, and the like, the truth of which no one of sound mind ever seriously doubted; but because, from a close consideration of them, one realises that they are neither so strong nor clear as the reasonings which lead us to the knowledge of our mind and of God; so that the latter are, of all which come under human knowledge, the most certain and manifest—a conclusion which it was my single aim in these Meditations to establish; on this account I here omit mention of the various other questions which, in the course of the discussion, I also had occasion to consider.

. . . .

Meditation I. Of the Things of which we may Doubt

Let us suppose that we are asleep, and that all these particulars — namely the opening of the eyes, the motion of the head, the extending of the hands — are merely illusions; and even that we really possess neither a body nor hands such as we see. Nevertheless, it must be admitted at least that the objects which appear to us in sleep are, as it were, painted representations which could not have been formed unless in the likeness of realities; and, therefore, that those general objects, at all events — namely, eyes, a head, hands, and an entire body — are not simply imaginary, but really existent. For, in truth, painters themselves, even when they try to represent sirens and satyrs by forms the most fantastic and extraordinary, cannot bestow upon them forms and natures absolutely new, but can only make a certain mixture and composition of the limbs of different animals; or if they chance to imagine something so novel that nothing at all similar has ever been seen before, and such as is, therefore, purely fictitious and absolutely false, it is at least certain that the colours of which this is composed are real.

And on the same principle, although these general objects, viz., eyes, a head, hands and the like, be imaginary, we must nevertheless admit that there are at least some other objects still more simple and universal than these, of which are formed, just as of certain real colours, all those images of things, whether true and real or false and fantastic, that are found in our thought.

To this class of objects belong corporeal nature in general and its extension; the shape of extended things, their quantity or size and their number, as also the place in, and the time during which, they exist, and other things of the same sort. It will not, therefore, perhaps be an unsound conclusion from this that physics, astronomy, medicine and all the other sciences that have for their end the consideration of composite objects, are very much subject to doubt and uncertainty; but that arithmetic, geometry and the other sciences of the same class, which regard merely the simplest and most general objects, and scarcely inquire whether or not these exist in nature, contain something that is certain and indubitable: for whether I am awake or dreaming, it remains true that two and three make five, and that a square never has more than four sides; nor does it seem possible that truths so obvious could fall under a suspicion of falsity or uncertainty.

Nevertheless, the belief that there is a God who is all-powerful and who created me, such as I am, has for a long time been in my mind. How, then do I know that he has not arranged that there should be no earth, or sky or any extended things or shape or size or place, but that all the same I should have perceptions of all things and should think that they do not exist otherwise than as I perceive them? And further, as I sometimes think that others are in error in matters of which they believe themselves to possess a perfect knowledge, it is possible that God has decided that I should be deceived each time I add together two and three, or number the sides of a square, or form some judgment still more simple, if any more simple indeed can be imagined. But perhaps God is not willing that I should be thus deceived, for he is said to be supremely good. If, however, it were repugnant to the goodness of God to have created me subject to constant deception, it would seem likewise to be contrary to his goodness to allow me to be occasionally deceived; and yet it is clear that this is permitted. Some, indeed, might perhaps be found who would prefer to deny the existence of a being so powerful than to believe that everything else is uncertain. But let us not oppose their opinion for the moment, but suppose, as they would, that everything that has been said about God is a fiction: nevertheless, in whatever way they suppose that I reached the state in which I exist, whether by fate, or chance, or by an endless series of antecedents and consequents, or by any other means, it is clear (since to be deceived and to err is a kind of imperfection) that the less powerful the cause to which they assign my origin, the more probable it will be that I am imperfect enough to be deceived constantly. To these arguments I have assuredly nothing to reply, but am forced to declare that there is nothing at all that I formerly believed to be true which I could not now doubt, not in any light or unconsidered way, but from cogent and maturely considered reasons; so that henceforward I must stop and suspend judgment on these thoughts, and not assent to them any more readily than to those things that seem evidently false, if I am to discover anything fixed and certain in the sciences.

. . . .

I will suppose, then, not that God, who is sovereignly good and the fountain of truth, but that some malignant demon, who is at once exceedingly potent and deceitful, has employed all his artifice to deceive me; I will suppose that the sky, the air, the earth, colours, shapes, sounds, and all external things, are nothing better than illusion and deceit, by means of which this being has laid snares for my credulity; I will consider myself as without hands, eyes, flesh, blood, or any of the senses, and as falsely believing that I am possessed of these; I will continue resolutely fixed in this belief, and if indeed by this means it be not in my power to arrive at the knowledge of truth, I shall at least do what is in my power, viz. suspend my judgment and guard with settled purpose against giving my assent to what is false, and being imposed upon by this deceiver, whatever his power and artifice.

. . . .

Meditation II

. . . .

Let us consider the objects that are commonly thought to be the most distinctly known, the bodies we touch and

see; I do not mean bodies in general, for these general
notions are usually more confused, but some particular
body. Take, for example, this piece of wax which has just
been taken from the beehive; it has not yet lost the sweetness of the honey it contained; it still retains some of the
odour of the flowers from which it was gathered; its colour, shape, size are apparent, it is hard, cold, easily handled; and when struck with the finger it produces a sound;
everything that contributes to make a body as distinctly
known as possible, is found in the one before us. But while
I am speaking, let it be placed near the fire—what remains
of the taste evaporates, the smell disappears, it loses its
shape, its size increases, it becomes liquid, it grows hot,
it can hardly be handled, and when struck emits no sound.
Does the same wax still remain after this change? It must
be admitted that it does remain: no one doubts it or judges
otherwise. What, then, was it I knew with so much distinctness in the piece of wax? Certainly it can be nothing
of all that I observed by means of the senses, since all of
the things that fell under taste, smell, sight, touch and
hearing are changed, and yet the same wax remains. It
was perhaps what I now think, viz., that this was neither
the sweetness of honey, the pleasant odour of flowers, the
whiteness, the size nor the sound, but only a body that a
little before appeared to me under these forms and which
is now perceived under others. But what is it precisely
that I imagine when I think of it in this way? Let us consider it carefully and, putting aside all that does not belong
to the wax, see what remains. There certainly remains
nothing except something extended, flexible and moveable.
But what is meant by flexible and moveable? Is it that I
imagine the piece of wax, being round, to be incapable of
becoming square, or of passing from a square to a tri-
angular shape? Assuredly this is not the case, because I
conceive that it admits of an infinity of similar changes, but
I am unable to compass this infinity by imagination; consequently this conception which I have of the wax is not
the product of the faculty of imagination. But what now
is this extension? Is it not also unknown? For it becomes
greater when the wax is melting, greater when it has

melted, and greater still when the heat goes on increasing; and I should not conceive, clearly and according to truth, the wax as it is if I did not suppose that it admitted even a wider variety of extension than I ever imagined. I must, therefore, admit that by imagination I cannot conceive what the piece of wax is, and that it is the mind alone that conceives it: I speak of one piece in particular; for, as to wax in general, this is still more evident. But what is the piece of wax that can be conceived only by the mind or understanding? It is certainly the same that I see, touch, imagine, and the same that I know from the beginning. But (and this it is of importance to notice) the perception of it is neither an act of sight, of touch, nor of imagination, and never was, though it might formerly seem so, but is simply an intuition of the mind, which may be imperfect and confused, as it formerly was, or very clear and distinct, as it is at present, according as the attention is more or less directed to the elements which it contains, and of which it is composed.

.   .   .   .

But, finally, what shall I say of the mind itself, that is, of myself? for as yet I do not admit that I am anything but mind. What, then! I who seem to possess so distinct an apprehension of the piece of wax,—do I not know myself, both with greater truth and certitude, and also much more distinctly and clearly? For if I judge that the wax is or exists because I see it, it assuredly follows, much more evidently, that I myself am or exist, for the same reason; for it is possible that what I see may not in truth be wax, and that I do not even possess eyes with which to see anything; but it cannot be that when I see, or, which comes to the same thing, when I think I see, I myself who think am nothing. So likewise, if I judge that the wax exists because I touch it, it will still also follow that I am; and if I determine that my imagination, or any other cause, whatever it be, persuades me of the existence of the wax, I will still draw the same conclusion. And what I have remarked here about the piece of wax can be applied to all the other things that are external to me. And further, if the notion or knowledge of wax appeared to me more pre-

cise and distinct, after not only sight and touch, but many
other causes besides, with how much greater distinctness
must I now know myself, since all the reasons that contribute to the knowledge of the nature of wax, or of any
body whatever, manifest still better the nature of my mind?
And there are besides so many other things in the mind
itself that contribute to the illustration of its nature, that
those dependent on the body, to which I have here referred, scarcely merit to be taken into account.

But, in conclusion, I find I have, without noticing it,
returned to the point I intended; for, since it is now manifest to me that bodies themselves are not properly perceived by the senses nor by the faculty of imagination, but
by the intellect alone; and since we do not know them
because we see them, or because we touch them, but
solely because we conceive them in thought, I readily discover that there is nothing more easily or clearly apprehended than my own mind. . . .

Meditation III

I will now close my eyes, I will stop my ears, I will turn
away my senses, I will even efface from my consciousness
all the images of corporeal things; or at least, because this
can hardly be accomplished, I will consider them as empty
and false; and thus, holding converse only with myself,
and closely examining my inner self, I will try to obtain
by degrees a more intimate and familiar knowledge of
myself. I am a thinking (conscious) thing, that is, a being
who doubts, affirms, denies, knows little, and is ignorant
of much, who loves, hates, wills, refuses, who imagines
and perceives; for, as I remarked before, although the
things which I perceive or imagine are perhaps nothing
at all apart from me and in themselves, I am nevertheless
sure that those modes of consciousness which I call perceptions and imaginations, in as far only as they are modes
of consciousness, exist in me. And in the little I have said
I think I have summed up all that I really know, or at least
all that up to this time I have discovered that I know. Now,
I will consider more exactly whether I can still discover in
myself some further knowledge which I have not yet ob-

served. I am certain that I am a thinking thing; but do I not therefore likewise know what is required to render me certain of a truth? In this first knowledge, doubtless, there is nothing that gives me assurance of its truth except the clear and distinct perception of what I affirm, which would not indeed be sufficient to give me the assurance that what I say is true, if it could ever happen that anything I thus clearly and distinctly perceived should prove false; and accordingly it seems to me that I may now take as a general rule, that all that is very clearly and distinctly conceived is true.

. . . .

Of my thoughts some are, as it were, images of things and to these alone properly belongs the name idea; as when I have before my mind a man, a chimera, the sky, an angel, or even God. Others, again, have certain other forms; as when I will, fear, affirm, or deny, I always indeed conceive something as the object of my thought, but I also add something to the idea I have of two objects; and of this class of thoughts some are called volitions or affections, and other judgments.

Now, with respect to ideas, if these are considered only in themselves, and are not referred to any object beyond them, they cannot, properly speaking, be false; for whether I imagine a goat or a chimera, it is not less true that I imagine the one than the other. Nor need we fear that falsity may exist in the will or affections; for, although I may desire objects that are wrong, and even that never existed, it is still true that I desire them. There thus remain only judgments, in which I must take great care not to be deceived. But the chief error that arises in them consists in judging that the ideas that are in us are like, or conform to, the things that are external to us; for assuredly, if we but considered the ideas themselves as certain modes of our thought, without referring them to anything beyond, they would hardly afford any occasion of error.

But, among these ideas, some appear to me to be innate, others adventitious, and others to be made by myself (factitious); for, as I have the power of conceiving what is called a thing, or a truth, or a thought, it seems to me that I

have this power from no other source than my own nature;
but if I now hear a noise, if I see the sun, or if I feel heat, I
have all along judged that these sensations proceeded from
certain objects existing outside myself; and it appears to me
that sirens, hippogryphs, and the like, are inventions of
my own mind. But I may even perhaps come to believe
that all my ideas are of the class that I call adventitious,
or that they are all innate, or that they are all factitious, for
I have not yet clearly discovered their true origin; and what
I have here principally to do is to consider, with reference
to those that appear to come from certain objects without
me, what grounds there are for thinking that they are like
these objects.

.   .   .   .

Meditation IV

I have accustomed myself these past days to separating
my mind from the senses, and I have accurately observed
that there is exceedingly little that is known with certainty
respecting corporeal objects,—that we know much more of
the human mind, and still more of God himself. I am thus
able now without difficulty to abstract my mind from the
contemplation of sensible or imaginable objects, and apply
it to those which, being free from all matter, are purely
intelligible. And certainly the idea I have of the human mind
in so far as it is a thinking thing, and not extended in length,
breadth, and depth, and participating in none of the properties of body, is incomparably more distinct than the idea
of any corporeal object; and when I consider that I doubt,
in other words, that I am an incomplete and dependent
being, the idea of a complete and independent being, that
is to say of God, occurs to my mind with so much clearness
and distinctness,—and from the fact alone that this idea
is found in me, or that I who possess it exist, the conclusions
that God exists, and that my own existence, each moment
of its continuance, is absolutely dependent upon him, are
so manifest,—as to lead me to believe it impossible that the
human mind can know anything with more clearness and
certitude. And now I seem to discover a path that will
conduct us from the contemplation of the true God, in

whom are contained all the treasures of science and wisdom, to the knowledge of the other things in the universe.

For, in the first place, I recognise that it is impossible for him ever to deceive me, for in all fraud and deceit there is a certain imperfection; and although it may seem that the ability to deceive is a mark of subtlety or power, yet the will to deceive provides unquestionable evidence of malice and weakness; and such, accordingly, cannot be found in God. In the next place, I experience in myself a certain faculty of judgment which I undoubtedly received from God, along with whatever else is mine; and since it is impossible that he should will to deceive me, it is likewise certain that he has not given me a faculty that will lead me into error, so long as I use it aright.

.   .   .   .

Whence, then, spring my errors? They arise from this cause alone, that I do not restrain the will, which is of much wider range than the understanding, within the same limits, but extend it even to things I do not understand, and, as the will is of itself indifferent to them, it readily falls into error and sin by choosing the false instead of the true, and evil instead of good.

For example, when I lately considered whether anything really existed in the world, and found that because I considered this question, it very manifestly followed that I myself existed, I could not but judge that what I so clearly conceived was true, not that I was forced to this judgment by any external cause, but simply because great clearness of the understanding was succeeded by strong inclination in the will; and I believed this just as much the more freely as I was less indifferent with respect to it. But now I not only know that I exist, in so far as I am a thinking being, but there is likewise presented to my mind a certain idea of corporeal nature; hence I am in doubt as to whether the thinking nature which is in me, or rather that by which I am what I am, is different from that corporeal nature, or whether both are merely one and the same thing. Here I suppose that I am as yet ignorant of any reason that would determine me to adopt the one belief in preference to the other: whence it happens that it is a matter of perfect in-

difference to me which of the two suppositions I affirm or
deny, or whether I form any judgment at all in the matter.

This indifference, moreover, extends not only to things
of which the understanding has no knowledge at all, but
in general also to all those which it does not discover with
perfect clearness at the moment the will is deliberating upon
them; for, however probable the conjectures may be that
dispose me to form a judgment in a particular matter,
the simple knowledge that these are merely conjectures,
and not certain and indubitable reasons, makes it possible
for me to form one that is directly the opposite. Of this I
lately had abundant experience, when I laid aside as false
all that I had before held for true, on the single ground that
I could in some degree doubt of it. But if I abstain from
judging of a thing when I do not conceive it with sufficient
clearness and distinctness, it is plain that I act rightly, and
am not deceived; but if I resolve to deny or affirm, I then
do not make a right use of my free will; and if I affirm what
is false, it is evident that I am deceived: moreover, even if
I judge in accordance with the truth, I stumble upon it by
chance, and do not therefore escape the imputation of a
wrong use of my freedom; for it is a dictate of the natural
light, that the knowledge of the understanding ought always
to precede the determination of the will.

.   .   .   .

Meditation V

.   .   .   .

Whatever proof or argument I use, it always returns
to this, that it is only the things I clearly and distinctly
conceive that have the power of completely persuading me.
And although, of the objects I conceive in this manner,
some, indeed, are obvious to every one, while others are
only discovered after close and careful investigation; nevertheless, after they are once discovered, the latter are not
esteemed less certain than the former. Thus, for example,
to take the case of the right-angled triangle, although it is
not so manifest at first that the square of the base is equal
to the squares of the other two sides, as that the base is
opposite to the greatest angle; nevertheless, after it is once
apprehended, we are as firmly persuaded of the truth of

the former as of the latter. And, with respect to God, if I were not preoccupied by prejudices, and my thoughts distracted by the continual presence of the images of sensible objects, I should know nothing sooner or more easily than the fact of his being. For is there any truth more clear than the existence of a Supreme Being, or of God, seeing it is to his essence alone that necessary and eternal existence pertains? And although the right conception of this truth has cost me much close thinking, nevertheless at present I feel not only as assured of it as of what I deem most certain, but I remark further that the certitude of all other truths is so absolutely dependent on it, that without this knowledge it is impossible ever to know anything perfectly.

Although I am of such a nature as to be unable, while I possess a very clear and distinct apprehension of a matter, to resist the conviction of its truth, yet because I am also of such a nature that I cannot keep my mind continually fixed on the same object, and as I frequently recollect having judged a thing to be true without recalling the reasons that made me so judge it, it may happen meanwhile that other reasons are presented to me which would readily cause me to change my opinion, if I did not know that God existed; and so I should possess no true and certain knowledge, but merely vague and vacillating opinions. Thus, for example, when I consider the nature of the triangle, it most clearly appears to me, who know little of the principles of geometry, that its three angles are equal to two right angles, and I find it impossible to believe otherwise, while I apply my mind to the proof; but as soon as I cease from attending to the process of proof, although I still remember that I had a clear comprehension of it, yet I may readily come to doubt of the truth demonstrated, if I do not know that there is a God: for I may persuade myself that I have been so constituted by nature as to be sometimes deceived, even in matters which I think I apprehend with the greatest evidence and certitude, especially when I recollect that I frequently considered many things to be true and certain which other reasons afterwards compelled me to reckon as wholly false.

But after I have discovered that God exists, since I at the same time observed that all things depend on him, and that he is no deceiver, and inferred from this that everything I clearly and distinctly perceive is of necessity true: although I no longer attend to the grounds of a judgment, no opposite reason can be alleged sufficient to lead me to doubt of its truth, provided only I remember that I once possessed a clear and distinct comprehension of it. My knowledge of it thus becomes true and certain. And this same knowledge extends similarly to whatever I remember to have formerly demonstrated, such as the truths of geometry and the like; for what can be alleged against them to lead me to doubt of them? Will it be that my nature is such that I may be frequently deceived? But I already know that I cannot be deceived in judgments of the grounds of which I possess a clear knowledge. Will it be that I formerly considered things to be true and certain which I afterwards discovered to be false? But I had no clear and distinct knowledge of any of those things, and, being as yet ignorant of the rule by which I am assured of the truth of a judgment, I was led to give my assent to them on grounds which I afterwards discovered were less strong than at the time I imagined them to be. What further objection, then, is there? Will it be said that perhaps I am asleep (an objection I lately myself raised), or that all the thoughts of which I am now conscious have no more truth than the reveries of my dreams? But although, in truth, I should be dreaming, the rule still holds that all which is clearly presented to my intellect is indisputably true.

And thus I very clearly see that the certitude and truth of all knowledge depends only on the knowledge of the true God, insomuch that, before I knew him, I could have no perfect knowledge of anything else. And now that I know him, I possess the means of acquiring a perfect knowledge about things, not only those that are in him, but also those connected with corporeal nature, in so far as it can serve as the subject of geometrical demonstrations, which do not concern themselves with the question whether it exists or not.

Meditation VI

There now only remains the inquiry as to whether material things exist. With regard to this question, I at least know with certainty that such things may exist, in as far as they constitute the subject of geometrical demonstrations, since, regarding them in this aspect, I can conceive them clearly and distinctly. For there can be no doubt that God possesses the power of producing all the objects I am able distinctly to conceive, and I never considered anything impossible to him, except when I found a contradiction in the attempt to conceive it aright. Further, the faculty of imagination which I possess, and of which I am conscious that I make use when I apply myself to the consideration of material things, is sufficient to persuade me of their existence: for, when I attentively consider what imagination is, I find that it is simply a certain application of the faculty of knowledge to a body which is immediately present to it, and which therefore exists.

And to render this quite clear, I remark in the first place, the difference there is between imagination and pure intellect. For example, when I imagine a triangle I not only conceive that it is a figure bounded by three lines, but at the same time also I look upon these three lines as present by the power and internal application of my mind, and this is what I call imagining. But if I want to think of a chiliogon, I indeed rightly conceive that it is a figure composed of a thousand sides, as easily as I conceive that a triangle is a figure composed of only three sides; but I cannot imagine the thousand sides of a chiliogon as I do the three sides of a triangle, nor, so to speak, view them as present with my mind's eyes. And although, in accordance with the habit I have of always imagining something when I think of corporeal things, it may happen that, in conceiving a chiliogon, I confusedly represent some figure to myself, yet it is quite evident that this is not a chiliogon, since it in no wise differs from that which I would represent to myself, if I were to think of a myriogon, or any other figure of many sides; nor would this reprensentation be of any use in discovering the properties that constitute the difference between a chili-

ogon and other polygons. But if it is a question of considering a pentagon, it is quite true that I can conceive its
figure, as well as that of a chiliogon, without the aid of imagination; but I can likewise imagine it by applying the
attention of my mind to its five sides, and at the same time
to the area which they contain. Thus I observe that a special
effort of mind is necessary to the act of imagination, which
is not required to conceiving or understanding; and this
special exertion of mind clearly shows the difference between imagination and pure intellect. I notice, besides,
that this power of imagination which I possess, in as far as
it differs from the power of conceiving, is in no way necessary to my nature or essence, that is, to the essence of my
mind; even if I did not possess it, I should still remain
the same that I now am, from which it seems we may conclude that it depends on something different from my mind.
And I easily conceive that, if some body exists, with which
my mind is so conjoined and united as to be able, as it
were, to consider it when it chooses, it may thus imagine
corporeal objects; so that this mode of thinking differs from
pure intellect only in this respect, that the mind in conceiving turns in some way upon itself, and considers some
one of the ideas it possesses within itself; but in imagining
it turns towards the body, and contemplates in it some
object that conforms to the idea which it either conceived
in itself or apprehended by the senses. I easily understand,
I say, that imagination may be thus formed, if it is true that
there are bodies; and because I find no other obvious mode
of explaining it, I thence, with probability, conjecture that
they exist, but only with probability; and although I carefully examine all things, nevertheless I do not find that,
from the distinct idea of corporeal nature I have in my
imagination, I can necessarily infer the existence of any
body.

.   .   .   .

. . . I find in myself a certain passive faculty of perception, that is, of receiving and taking knowledge of the ideas
of sensible things; but this would be useless to me, if there
did not also exist in me, or in some other thing, another
active faculty capable of forming and producing those ideas.

But this active faculty cannot be in me in as far as I am but a thinking thing, seeing that it does not presuppose thought, and also that those ideas are frequently produced in my mind without my contributing to them in any way, and even frequently contrary to my will. This faculty must therefore exist in some substance different from me, in which all the objective reality of the ideas that are produced by this faculty is contained formally or eminently, as I before remarked: and this substance is either a body, that is to say, a corporeal nature in which is contained formally all that is objectively and by representation in those ideas; or it is God himself, or some other creature, of a rank superior to body, in which the same is contained eminently. But as God is no deceiver, it is manifest that he does not of himself and immediately communicate those ideas to me, nor even by the intervention of any creature in which their objective reality is not formally, but only eminently, contained. For as he has given me no faculty whereby I can discover this to be the case, but, on the contrary, a very strong inclination to believe that those ideas arise from corporeal objects, I do not see how he could be vindicated from the charge of deceit, if, in fact, they proceeded from some other source, or were produced by causes other than corporeal things: and accordingly it must be concluded that corporeal objects exist. Nevertheless they are not perhaps exactly such as we perceive by the senses, for their comprehension by the senses is, in many instances, very obscure and confused; but it is at least necessary to admit that everything I clearly and distinctly conceive as in them, that is, generally speaking, everything contained in the object of speculative geometry, really exists external to me.

.   .   .   .

. . . And I ought to reject all the doubts of those bygone days as exaggerated and ridiculous, especially that general uncertainty respecting sleep, which I could not distinguish from the waking state: for I now find a very marked difference between the two states, in that our memory can never connect our dreams with each other and with the course of life, in the way it constantly does with events that occur when we are awake. And, in fact, if some one,

when I was awake, appeared to me all of a sudden and
suddenly disappeared, as do the images I see in sleep, so
that I could not observe either where he came from or
where he went, it would be quite reasonable for me to
think it a spectre or phantom formed in my brain, rather
than a real man. But when I perceive objects with regard
to which I can distinctly determine both where they come
from, and where they are, and the time at which they appear to me, and when, without interruption, I can connect the perception I have of them with the whole of the
other parts of my life, I am perfectly sure that what I thus
perceive occurs while I am awake and not during sleep.
And I ought not in the least degree to doubt of the truth
of those presentations, if, after having called together all
my senses, my memory, and my understanding to examine
them by any one of these faculties which is repugnant to
that of any other: for since God is no deceiver, it necessarily follows that I am not herein deceived. But because
the necessities of action frequently oblige us to come to a
decision before we have had leisure for so careful an
examination, it must be confessed that the life of man is
liable to frequent error with respect to individual objects;
and we must, in conclusion, acknowledge the weakness of
our nature.}

CHAPTER V

Pascal

BLAISE PASCAL WAS BORN IN 1623 AND DIED IN 1662. HE was perhaps the most brilliant and profound Christian apologist that Europe has known since the Middle Ages. He was a great mathematician and a great thinker, but he was not an original philosopher, in the narrower sense of that word; for he was not primarily concerned to construct a systematic theory of knowledge or a rational scheme of reality. He wished only to show the inevitable weakness of human reason and the necessity of faith.

In the *Pensées* he describes, with unequaled force of language and psychological insight, the various phases of human despair, uncertainty and sense of unworthiness. But he asserts also the power and dignity of human thought, which at least makes men realize their own imperfection. This power to grasp his own imperfection is the greatness of man.

There is a peculiar vividness and tension in Pascal's writing; he himself had abandoned the study of mathematics for religious meditation, after showing great genius in his mathematical inventions. He invented a calculating machine and contributed to the theory of chance. No one was in a better position to understand the power of reason; in the two famous extracts from the *Pensées* printed below, he affirms the dignity of the human soul against the background of the new cosmology which was showing the immensities of the physical universe.

The original French is preserved, with a translation attached, because the words, as he wrote them, have their own force and place in history.

[CHAPTER XXIII. *Grandeur de l'Homme*

L'homme n'est qu'un roseau, le plus faible de la nature;
mais c'est un roseau pensant. Il ne faut pas que l'univers
entier s'arme pour l'écraser: une vapeur, une goutte d'eau,
suffit pour le tuer. Mais, quand l'univers l'écraserait,
l'homme serait encore plus noble que ce qui le tue, parce
qu'il sait qu'il meurt, et l'avantage que l'univers a sur lui;
l'univers n'en sait rien.

Toute notre dignité consiste donc en la pensée. C'est
de là qu'il faut nous relever et non de l'espace et de la
durée, que nous ne saurions remplir. Travaillons donc à
bien penser: voilà le principe de la morale.

Man is only a reed, the weakest to be found in nature;
but he is a thinking reed. It is not necessary for the whole
of nature to take up arms to crush him: a puff of smoke,
a drop of water, is enough to kill him. But, even if the
universe should crush him, man would still be more noble
than that which destroys him, because he knows that he
dies and he realises the advantage which the universe
possesses over him. The universe knows nothing of this.

All our dignity, then, consists in thought. It is upon this
that we must depend, not on space and time, which we
would not in any case be able to fill. Let us labour, then, to
think well: this is the foundation of morality.

Appendix to Chapter XXIII

Roseau pensant.— Ce n'est point de l'espace que je dois
chercher ma dignité, mais c'est du règlement de ma pensée.
Je n'aurai pas d'avantage en possédant des terres: par
l'espace, l'univers me comprend et m'engloutit comme un
point; par la pensée, je le comprends.

Thinking reed.—It is not in space that I should look to
find my dignity, but rather in the ordering of my thought.
I would gain nothing further by owning territories: in
point of space the universe embraces me and swallows me
up like a mere point: in thought, I embrace the universe.]

CHAPTER VI

Spinoza

BARUCH SPINOZA WAS BORN IN AMSTERDAM IN 1632 INTO a prosperous Jewish commercial family, which had come to Holland from Portugal in the sixteenth century. He was first educated at a Jewish school and spent his childhood and youth in the important Jewish community of Amsterdam. As a young man he came to know a circle of free-thinkers interested in philosophy, who profoundly respected his gifts as a philosopher. His growing reputation as a freethinking philosopher led to his formal exclusion from the Jewish community in 1656. He was formally cursed and no Jew was to have any intercourse with him of any kind. For the remainder of his life he lived alone in various places in Holland, separated from the Jewish community; he was visited by, and corresponded with, a small circle of friends who knew of his philosophical work, most of which could not be published in his lifetime. He earned his living by grinding and polishing lenses. He corresponded with Oldenburg, Secretary of the Royal Society in London, and his work was known to Huygens, Boyle and other natural philosophers, and, although he lived in retirement from the world, his liberal attitude in politics became widely known. In 1665 he is believed to have intervened on the side of the de Witts by accepting a secret mission to the French. For reasons set out in his *Tractatus Theologico-Politicus,* he was an enemy of all persecuting churches, not excluding the Calvinists, who were active in Holland and who accepted the leadership of William of Orange. Like Hobbes, he wished to strengthen the secular power of the state against the warring, persecuting Christian churches; he demanded a purely secular state, which would be indifferent in matters of religious doctrine. He was the first great philosophical advocate of toleration in the modern spirit. He refused an offer from the Elector Palatine at Heidelberg to teach philosophy, under conditions of complete freedom, at the University of Heidelberg; he explained that as a philosopher he preferred to remain free of public commitments. He had conversations with Leibniz, who visited him and subsequently denounced his dangerous errors. To know Spinoza was in itself dangerous, so great was his reputation as an implacable atheist and freethinker. He died of consumption in 1677, having suffered from this disease for many years.

The only work to be published under his own name in his lifetime was the *Principles of Descartes's Philosophy,* together with an appendix called *Metaphysical Thoughts.* This is an exposition of Descartes's philosophy in geometrical order, and does not present his own thought. The *Theological-Political Treatise* was published anonymously in 1670 under a false imprint, and aroused scandal and hostility because of its skepticism about religious doctrine. That Spinoza was the author was generally known or inferred. Spinoza's masterpiece, the *Ethics,* plainly could not be published in his lifetime. After his death his friends produced his works in a single volume, which included the *Ethics, On the Improvement of Understanding, Treatise on Politics,* and his learned correspondence. The *Ethics* was condemned as atheistical and morally subversive, and was largely neglected until towards the end of the eighteenth century when Goethe, and later Shelley, Coleridge and other romantic writers, aroused interest in Spinoza.

Throughout the nineteenth century Spinoza was admired, if not always understood, from many different points of view: by some he was represented as a materialist and rationalist critic of established morality, by others as a mystical pantheist. He was rightly seen as a precursor of the Higher Criticism of the Bible, and as an advocate of liberalism and toleration. Some of the origins of his thought have been found in earlier Jewish philosophy; on the other hand some scholars have interpreted his philosophy as

solely a development of Descartes's. These interpretations
are partial and incomplete. It is true that Spinoza was
deeply influenced by the moral and intellectual traditions
of the Jews, and it is true that his thought started from
Descartes's conclusions and that he never abandoned
Descartes's canons of clarity and deductive rigor. But,
unlike Descartes, he was above all a moralist, who based
his doctrine of the true salvation of man, and of the nature of society, on a metaphysical scheme which showed
man's place in nature.

The following extracts do not include anything of the
moral psychology, which is the subject of Parts III and
IV of the *Ethics,* or of the picture of the free man, which is
the subject of Part V. These extracts present only the
main outlines of Spinoza's metaphysical system, which in
the *Ethics* was set out in geometrical order, partly to achieve
the greatest rigor and clarity that the subject admits, partly
in order to achieve impersonality and detachment. In fact
the argument does not, and indeed could not, follow a
strictly deductive pattern, in which each step can be justified by reference to the previous proposition. Spinoza
argues that there can be only a single substance, God or
Nature, which necessarily exists and is the cause of itself;
all other things or aspects of reality must be explained as
attributes or modes of this single substance. There cannot
be a Creator who is distinct from his creation; God or
Nature must be eternally self-creating. Nor can there be
any ultimate distinction between two substances, or quasi-
substances, Mind and Matter (or Extension), as Descartes had supposed; thought and the system of things in
space are only two aspects of the single reality, and are at
every point inseparable. All particular things, including
human things, must be thought of as having their determined place in the system of causes in Nature. As we
advance in knowledge of the true order of causes in Nature, we realize that nothing in the world could possibly
be other than it is. Spinoza was an uncompromising deter-
minist, and he represented every human choice, attitude,
or feeling as the necessary effect of causes in the infinite
chain of causes. A man is no less a part of Nature than any

other natural object, and his actions and reactions are to
be studied and improved in a spirit of scientific detachment; most ordinary moral condemnation and exhorta-
tion is a mark of ignorance, and of not understanding the
causes of human passions and actions. It was this deter-
minism in the sphere of morality and human choice that
seemed subversive to Spinoza's contemporaries, together
with his identification of God with Nature.

Spinoza's argument in the *Ethics* turns on the notions
of Cause and Substance and on the assumption that everything must have some rational explanation. In the order
of explanation we must finally acknowledge something
which is the cause of itself, the ultimate, terminating cause;
but this substance can be nothing but God or Nature as
a whole. In the development of this central notion there
is much that is profoundly obscure, and one may read
Spinoza's *Ethics* many times, as did his contemporaries,
and still come back to some unsolved problems of interpretation. What is the relation of the two Infinite Attributes
of Thought and Extension to each other? Why is God or
Nature conceived by us under just these two Attributes?
In what sense is everything in Nature to some degree ani-
mated? Is the existence and nature of the various finite
modes, which are particular things, somehow deducible
from the universal features of Nature, or is deduction confined to the eternal modes of Nature? What is the place
allowed to experiment in natural knowledge? These are
but a few of the many questions which a Spinozist must
answer. But at least the outlines of this truly systematic
philosophy are plain, and its vision of a complete knowledge of the necessary scheme of the natural order, infinite, eternal and self-creating, in which man can be free
by understanding the true order of nature and so detach-
ing himself from his transitory interests. Physics and medicine, including psychology, are the useful sciences, and all
problems are soluble by the use of reason, which is the
true happiness of man. In the *Tractatus Theologico-Politicus* he applied his metaphysical principles to the interpretation of religious belief and the problems of politics. He
showed how the free man, who is a genuine philosopher,

would behave as a citizen and in relation to the established church. And he advocated tolerance and liberalism as the necessary condition of any individual enlightenment.

Spinoza's main concern was with his moral philosophy; but he sought to demonstrate it as following directly from certain metaphysical views. It is with the latter that these extracts are concerned; they are drawn from Books I and II of the *Ethics,* which contain, in germ, the metaphysical view of the world from which Spinoza's doctrine of human bondage and of human freedom follow. These comments will mention only a few of his leading notions.

Spinoza's philosophy is in many ways the opposite of Leibniz's. Both are concerned with the notion of substance, but whereas Leibniz considers that there must be numberless substances, all different, Spinoza holds that there can be only one. Leibniz's God is the Creator of his substances; Spinoza's God is identical with the One Substance. Leibniz's God is a free agent who chooses between possibilities with a view to bringing about the best of all possible worlds; Spinoza denies that God can possess a Will, and considers the idea that all works for the best in human terms to be a vulgar superstition. Leibniz is not primarily concerned with the end of human action; he seeks to explain the nature of the universe, and merely finds free will of the traditional pattern which man enjoys. Spinoza allows no such freedom. His concern is with the struggle of the virtuous man to make himself free, by gaining an understanding of the nature and the origins of the passions from which he suffers. By arriving at knowledge of a higher order, a man can make himself free; for, as he gains knowledge, the passive ideas — the emotions — turn themselves into an active interest in eternal truths. All passionate interests in particular things are, for Spinoza, ultimately only a kind of misunderstanding: the failure to see the world as a whole and to grasp the essential connection of its internal necessities.

In Book I of the *Ethics* Spinoza sets up the structure of this world. He starts his definitions with the concept of something that is the cause of itself, with substance and with God. God is defined as a Being absolutely infinite,

a substance of infinite attributes. Substance is defined as
that the conception of which does not depend for its formation on anything else. This means that in replying to the
question "What is it?", one does not need to mention any
other being. Spinoza considers that the explanation of
anything involves mentioning its cause, that which makes
it what it is. Accordingly "the cause of itself" is defined as
that whose essence involves existence. As the explanation
of the existence of anything involves reference to its cause,
the explanation of the existence of something which is
cause of itself involves reference only to itself—i.e. its
essence involves existence or, when one realizes what it is,
one must realize that it exists.

These three concepts, God, Substance and Cause of
Itself, are now shown to be identical. The substance and
that which is cause of itself are seen to be identical in virtue
of their definitions and of Axioms 1 to 4. If the explanation of substance does not involve reference to anything
else, and the explanation of everything else does involve
such a reference, except in the case of that which is cause
of itself, evidently substance must be cause of itself. Substance is shown to be identical with God by means
of Proposition 8 —"all substance is infinite, i.e., has infinite attributes" (Propositions 9 and 10, note), and Proposition 7, which asserts the identity of substance with that
which is cause of itself and draws the conclusion that the
substance necessarily exists. Hence substance is a necessary
existent with infinite attributes, i.e., God. There can be
only one such substance (Proposition 14). This follows in
turn from Proposition 5, which shows that there cannot be
two or more substances with the same attribute, together
with the consideration that the ultimate explanation of
everything, provided by the existence of God, rests on His
attributes.

Spinoza distinguishes the attributes of God from the
affections or modes of these attributes. God has, as we
have seen, infinite attributes, and this includes the idea
that He has an infinite number of attributes. But the human
mind actually conceives God under only two attributes,
Thought and Extension; that is, all our explanations of

anything must come back to the single substance conceived either as a Thinking Thing or as an Extended Thing. Here Spinoza is in opposition to Descartes, who considered that there were two sorts of substance, thinking and extended substance. In Spinoza's system God comes to be *equated* with Nature, as the totality of things, each of which is to be understood as a modification of one of the two attributes of substance. God or Nature is eternal and self-creating.

Having given a priori proof of the existence of God, Spinoza gives also an a posteriori proof, which he considers independent. This proof has some similarities to Leibniz's argument in *The Ultimate Origin of Things,* from which an extract is given in Chapter VII. Here the argument is that any explanation of anything depends on stating its cause; so either there is an infinite regress of explanations, and therefore nothing is adequately explained at all, or there is a necessary Being, unless nothing exists at all. But evidently we exist, and some explanations are adequate, so there must be a necessary Being.

The core of this whole argument is that the universe, in order to be intelligible, must be conceived as a whole, and, as such, must be eternal, infinite, a single self-explaining system.

[Part I. *Concerning God: Definitions*

I. I understand that to be a Cause of Itself [*causa sui*] whose essence involves existence and whose nature cannot be conceived unless existing.

II. That thing is said to be Finite in Its Kind [*in suo genere finita*] which can be limited by another thing of the same kind. E.g., a body is said to be finite because we can conceive another larger than it. Thus a thought is limited by another thought. But a body cannot be limited by a thought, nor a thought by a body.

III. I understand Substance to be that which is in itself and is conceived through itself: I mean that, the conception of which does not depend on the conception of another thing from which it must be formed.

IV. An Attribute I understand to be that which the intellect perceives as constituting the essence of a substance.

V. By Mode I understand the Affections [*affectiones*] of a substance, or that which is in something else through which it may be conceived.

VI. God I understand to be a being absolutely infinite, that is, a substance consisting of infinite attributes, each of which expresses eternal and infinite essence.

Explanation. I say absolutely infinite, but not in its own kind. For, of whatever is infinite only in its own kind, we may deny an infinity of attributes, but to the essence of that which is absolutely infinite pertains everything that expresses essence and involves no denial.

VII. A thing is said to be Free which exists by the mere necessity of its own nature and is determined to act by itself alone. A thing is said to be Necessary, or rather Compelled, when it is determined to exist and to produce its effects by something else on a fixed and determined principle.

VIII. I understand Eternity to be existence itself, in so far as it is conceived to follow necessarily from the mere definition of an eternal thing.

Explanation. For such existence is conceived, like the essence of the thing, as an eternal truth; and therefore cannot be explained by duration or time, even if the duration is conceived as without beginning and end.

Axioms

I. All things, which are, are in themselves or in another thing.

II. That which cannot be conceived through another thing must be conceived through itself.

III. From a given determined cause an effect follows of necessity, and on the other hand, if no determined cause is granted, it is impossible that an effect should follow.

IV. The knowledge of effect depends on the knowledge of cause, and involves that knowledge.

V. Of two things that have nothing in common with each other, neither can be comprehended through the other.

VI. A true idea should agree with that of which it is the idea [*ideatum*].

VII. The essence of that which can be conceived as not existing does not involve existence.

Propositions

I. A substance is prior in its nature to its affections.

II. Two substances having different attributes have nothing in common with each other.

Proof. This is obvious from Def. 3. For each of them must be in itself and be conceived through itself; or, the conception of one of them does not involve the conception of the other.

III. Of two things having nothing in common with each other, one cannot be the cause of the other.

Proof. If they have nothing in common with each other, then (Ax. 5) they cannot be known through each other, and therefore (Ax. 4) one cannot be the cause of the other. Q.E.D.

IV. Two or more distinct things are distinguished one from the other by the difference of the attributes of the substance, or by the difference of their affections.

Proof. All things that are, are either in themselves or in other things (Ax. 1), that is (Defs. 3 and 5), outside the intellect, there is nothing save substances and their affections. Therefore there is nothing outside the intellect through which several things may be distinguished one from the other except substances, or, what is the same thing (Ax. 4), their attributes or affections. Q.E.D.

V. There cannot be in nature two or more substances having the same nature or attribute.

Proof. If several distinct substances were given, they would have to be distinguished one from another by the difference either of their attributes or of their affections. If they were to be distinguished just by the differences of their attributes, it would follow that there could not be granted two or more having the same attribute. Suppose, on the other hand, that they were to be distinguished by the difference of their affections; since a substance is prior in its nature to its affections, we may leave the affections outside, and consider the substance in itself, that is (Def. 3, Ax. 6), consider it truly; and then we could not conceive of it as distinct from another, that is (prev. Prop.) there could not be more than one substance possessing the same attributes. Q.E.D.

VI. One substance cannot be produced by another.

Proof. There cannot be in nature two substances with the same attribute (prev. Prop.), that is (Prop. 2), which have anything in common, and accordingly (Prop. 3) neither of them can be the cause of the other, or one cannot be produced by the other. Q.E.D.

Corollary. Hence it follows that a substance cannot be produced by anything else. For in the nature of things there is nothing save substances and their affections, as is obvious from Ax. 1 and Defs. 3 and 5; and substance cannot be produced by another substance (prev. Prop.). Therefore there is no way at all in which a substance could be produced by anything else. Q.E.D.

VII. Existence pertains to the nature of substance.

Proof. A substance cannot be produced by anything else (prev. Prop. Coroll.): it will therefore be its own cause, that is (Def. 1.), its essence necessarily involves existence, or existence pertains to its nature. Q.E.D.

VIII. All substance is necessarily infinite.

Proof. There can only be one substance that has any given attribute (Prop. 5) and it pertains to the nature of that substance that it should exist (Prop. 7). It must therefore exist either as finite or as infinite. But not as finite. For (Def. 2), it would then be limited by some other substance of the same nature, which would also necessarily have to exist (Prop. 7): and then two substances would be granted having the same attribute, which is absurd (Prop. 5). It exists, therefore, infinitely. Q.E.D.

Note 1. As to call anything finite is, really, in part, a denial, and to call it infinite is the absolute assertion of the existence of its nature, it follows therefore (from Prop. 7 alone) that all substance must be infinite.

Note 2. I do not doubt that to all those who are confused in their judgments about things, and are not accus-

tomed to know them by their first causes, it may be difficult to conceive the proof of the seventh Proposition; because, in fact, they do not distinguish between the modifications of substances and substances themselves, and do
not know how things are produced. The result is that
they ascribe to substances the origins that they see possessed
by things in nature. For those who do not know the real
causes of things confuse everything, and without the least
mental repugnance imagine trees speaking like men, and
that men can be conceived as made from stones as well
as from human seed, and imagine any form to be changed
into any other one likes. So also those who confuse divine
with human nature easily attribute human effects to God,
more especially while they do not know how effects are
produced in the mind. But if men would give heed to the
nature of substance they would not doubt at all the truth
of Prop. 7; rather everyone would consider it an axiom,
and it would take its place among common notions. For
by substance they would understand that which is in itself,
and is conceived through itself, or rather that the knowledge
of which does not depend on the knowledge of any other
thing; but by modification, that which is in something else,
and that the conception of which is formed from the conception of whatever it is in. Therefore we may have true
ideas of modifications which do not exist; since, although
they do not really exist outside the mind, yet their essence
is contained in something else in such a way that they may
be conceived through that thing. The truth of substances
does not exist outside the mind; they are conceived in themselves, because through themselves. If anyone should say,
then, that he has a clear and distinct, that is a true, idea
of substance, and should nevertheless doubt whether such
substance existed, he would indeed be like one who should
say that he has a true idea and yet should doubt whether it
were false (as will be manifest to anyone who pays a little
attention); or if anyone should say that substance was created, he would state at the same time that a false idea might
be made true; and it is difficult to conceive anything more
absurd than this. And therefore it must necessarily be ac-
knowledged that the existence of substance, like its essence,

is an eternal truth. And hence we may conclude, in another
manner, that there cannot be two substances of the same
nature: which it is now perhaps worth while to show. But
let me arrange this in its proper order. Therefore note (1)
the true definition of each thing involves nothing, and expresses nothing, but the nature of the thing defined. From
which it follows (2) that clearly no definition involves any
certain number of individuals, nor expresses it, since the
definition expresses nothing else than the nature of the
thing defined. E.g., the definition of a triangle expresses
nothing else than the simple nature of a triangle, but not
a certain number of triangles. Let it be noted again, (3),
that for each existing thing there is a cause by reason of
which it exists. Note, moreover, that the cause by reason
of which a thing exists should either be contained in the
very nature and definition of the existing thing (simply
because it pertains to its nature to exist), or should be
given outside it. It follows from these positions that, if a
certain number of individuals exist in nature, a cause must
necessarily be given why those individuals, and not more
or less, exist. E.g., if in nature twenty men were to exist
(whom, for the sake of clarity, I will suppose to exist at
the same time, and that none existed before them), it
would not be enough, when giving a reason of why twenty
men existed, to show the cause of human nature in general;
it would first be necessary to show the cause why not more
nor less than twenty existed: since (Note 3) a reason or
cause should be given why each one existed. But this cause
cannot be contained in human nature itself (Notes 2 and
3), since the true definition of man does not involve the
number twenty. Hence (Note 4) the reason why these
twenty men exist, and consequently why each one of them
exists, must necessarily be given outside each one of them:
and therefore we must conclude generally that whenever it
is possible for several individuals of the same nature to
exist, there must be an external cause for them in fact to
exist. Since, as has been shown already in this Note, existence pertains to the nature of substance, its definition must
of necessity involve existence, and therefore from its mere
definition its existence can be concluded. But since in

Notes 2 and 3 we have shown that from its definition the existence of several substances cannot follow, it follows necessarily therefore that two or more substances cannot have the same nature; as was asserted.

IX. The more reality or being a thing has, the more attributes belong to it.

X. Each attribute of one substance must be conceived through itself.

Proof. An attribute is that which the intellect perceives of a substance as constituting its essence (Def. 4), therefore (Def. 3) it must be conceived through itself. Q.E.D.

Note. Hence it appears that even though two attributes are conceived as really distinct, that is, one is conceived without the aid of the other, we cannot thence conclude that they form two entities or two different substances. For it follows from the nature of a substance that each of its attributes can be conceived through itself: for all the attributes it ever had were always in it at the same time, nor could one of them be produced from another, but each of them expresses the reality or being of the substance. Therefore it is far from being absurd to attribute several attributes to one substance; since nothing is more clear than that each entity should be conceived under some attribute, and the more reality or being it has, the more attributes expressing necessity, or eternity and infinity, belong to it; and also nothing can be clearer than that an entity must be defined as absolutely infinite (as we defined it in Def. 6), which consists of infinite attributes, each of which expresses a certain eternal and infinite essence. But if anyone asks by what sign we shall be able to know the difference of substances, let him read the following Propositions, which will show that in the nature of things only one substance exists, and that it is absolutely infinite; therefore he will ask for that sign in vain.

XI. God, or a substance consisting of infinite attributes, each of which expresses eternal and infinite essence, necessarily exists.

Proof. If you deny it, conceive, if it be possible, that God does not exist. Then (Ax. 7) his essence does not involve existence. But this (Prop. 7) is absurd. Therefore God necessarily exists. Q.E.D.

Another Proof. A cause or reason ought to be assigned for each thing, why it exists or why it does not. E.g., if a triangle exists, there must be a reason or cause for its existence; but if it does not exist, there must be a reason or cause which prevents it from existing or which takes its existence from it. Now this reason or cause must be contained in the nature of the thing, or outside it. E.g., the reason why a square circle does not exist is shown by its nature, just because it involves a contradiction. On the other hand, the existence of substance follows from its nature alone, for that involves existence (*vide* Prop. 7). But the reason why a circle or triangle exists, or why it does not exist, does not follow from their nature, but from the order of universal corporeal nature; for it is from this that it must follow either that a triangle necessarily exists or that it is impossible that it can now exist. But this is in itself obvious. From which it follows that that must of necessity exist concerning which there is no reason or cause which could prevent its existence. If, thus, there is no reason or cause which could prevent the existence of God, or take his existence from him, it must certainly be concluded that he does exist of necessity. But if there is such a reason or cause, it must be either in the nature of God or outside it, that is, in another substance or another nature. For if the reasons lay in another substance of the same nature, the existence of God would be by this very fact admitted. But the substance of another nature has nothing in common with God (Prop. 2), and therefore can neither give him existence nor take it from him. And since the reason or cause which would take existence from God cannot be outside divine nature, i.e., the nature of God, it must of necessity lie, if indeed God does not exist, in his own nature, and this would involve a contradiction. But to assert this of a being absolutely infinite and perfect in all things is absurd: therefore neither within God nor without him is there any cause or reason that could take his existence from him, and consequently God must necessarily exist. Q.E.D.

Another Proof. Inability to exist is want of power, and, on the other hand, ability to exist is power (as is self-evident). And if that which now necessarily exists consists only of finite things, then finite things are more powerful than an absolutely infinite being; and this, as is self-evident, is absurd. Therefore, either nothing exists, or an absolutely infinite being necessarily exists. But we exist, either in ourselves or in something else that necessarily exists (*vide* Ax. 1 and Prop. 7). Therefore a being absolutely infinite, that is (Def. 6) God, necessarily exists. Q.E.D.

Note. In this last proof I wished to show the existence of God a posteriori, so that it might the more easily be understood, and not because the existence of God does not follow a priori from the same grounds. For since ability to exist is power, it follows that the more reality belongs to the nature of anything, the more power it will have to exist; and accordingly a being absolutely infinite, or God, has an absolutely infinite power of existence from itself, and on that account absolutely exists. Many, however, perhaps will not be able to see the force of this proof easily, because they are accustomed to consider those things which flow from external causes, and of these, those which are quickly made, that is, which exist easily, they see perish easily; and on the other hand, they judge those things to be harder to make, i.e., not existing so easily, to which they find more attributes belong. But, in truth, to deliver them from these prejudices, I need not show here in what manner or by what reason this statement "that which is quickly made perishes speedily" is true; or even, in considering the whole of nature, whether all things are equally difficult or not; but it suffices to note that I do not speak here of things which are made from external causes, but of substances alone which cannot be produced from any external cause. For those things which are made from external causes, whether they consist of many parts or few, whatever perfection or reality they have is only there by reason of their external cause; and therefore their existence arises merely from the perfection of some external cause and not from their own. On the other hand, whatever perfection a substance may have is due to no external cause: therefore its existence must follow from its nature alone, which is nothing else than its essence. Perfection, then, does not take existence from a thing, but, on the contrary, gives it existence; but imperfection, on the other hand, takes it away; and so we cannot be more certain of the existence of anything than of the existence of a being absolutely infinite or perfect, that is, God. Since his essence excludes all imperfection, and involves absolute perfection, by that very fact it removes all cause of doubt concerning his existence and makes it most certain; which will be manifest, I think, to such as pay a little attention.

XII. No attribute of a substance can be truly conceived, from which it would follow that substance can be divided into parts.

XIII. Substance absolutely infinite is indivisible.

XIV. Except God, no substance can be granted or conceived.

Corollary 1. Hence it distinctly follows that God is one and unique, that is (Def. 6), there is in nature only one substance, and that it is absolutely infinite, as we intimated in the *Note* of Prop. 10.

Corollary 2. It follows, in the second place, that extension and thought are either attributes of God or affections of attributes of God. . . .

XVII. God acts merely according to his own laws, and is compelled by no one.

Corollary 1. Hence it follows that there is no cause, either within God or outside of him, that can incite him to act, except the perfection of his own nature.

Corollary 2. Hence it follows that God alone is a free cause. For God alone exists from the mere necessity of his own nature. (Prop. 11 and Coroll. 1, Prop. 14), and by the mere necessity of his nature, he acts (prev. Prop.). And therefore (Def. 7) he is the only free cause. Q.E.D.

Note. Others think that God is a free cause because they think he can bring it to pass that those things which we say follow from his nature, that is, which are in his power, should not come about, or that they should not be produced by him. But this is the same as if they said that God can

bring it to pass that it should not follow from the nature
of a triangle that its three angles are equal to two right
angles, or that from a given cause no effect should follow,
which is absurd. Further on, without the aid of this proposition, I shall show that intellect and will do not apper-
tain to the nature of God. I am well aware that there are
many who say they can show that the greatest intellect
and free will belong to the nature of God: for they say
they know nothing more perfect to attribute to God than
that which amongst us is the greatest perfection. Further,
although they conceive God as possessing in fact the highest intellect, yet they do not believe that he can, in fact,
bring about the existence of anything which is in his intellect: for they think they would thus destroy the power
of God. They say that if he had created everything that
is in his intellect, he would then not be able to create anything more, which they think opposed to the omnipotence
of God; and accordingly they prefer to consider God as
indifferent to all things, and as creating nothing except
what he determines to create by a certain absolute will.
But I think I have sufficiently shown (*vide* Prop. 16) that
from God's supreme power or infinite nature, infinite things
in infinite modes, that is all things, have necessarily flowed,
or always follow by the same necessity; in the same manner
as from the nature of a triangle it always has followed, and
always will follow, that its three angles should be equal to
two right angles. Wherefore God's omnipotence was actual
from eternity, and will remain in the same state of actuality
through all eternity. And in this manner, in my opinion,
the perfection of God's omnipotence is asserted to be far
greater. On the other hand, the opponents of God seem
to deny (to speak freely) his omnipotence. For they are
obliged to confess that God's intellect perceives many
things that could be created which nevertheless he cannot
ever create. For, in other words, if he created all that his
intellect perceived, he would, according to them, exhaust
his omnipotence and render himself imperfect. As, therefore, they say that God is perfect, they are reduced to
state at the same time that he cannot complete all those
things to which his power extends; and anything more

absurd than this, or more opposed to the omnipotence of
God, I cannot imagine could be conceived. Moreover (as
I would like to say something concerning the intellect and
will which we commonly attribute to God), if intellect
and will pertain to the eternal essence of God, something
far else must be understood by these two attributes than
what is commonly understood by men. For the intellect
and will that would constitute the essence of God must
differ *toto coelo* from our will and intellect, nor can they
agree in anything save name, any more than the dog, as a
heavenly body, and the dog, as a barking animal, agree.
This I shall show in the following manner. If intellect pertains to divine nature, it cannot, as with our intellect, be
posterior (as many suppose) or even simultaneous in nature with the things conceived by the intellect, since
(Coroll. 1, Prop. 16) God is prior in cause to all things;
but on the other hand, truth and the formal essence of
things is as it is, because it so exists objectively in God's
intellect. Wherefore the intellect of God, as far as it can
be conceived as forming his essence, is in truth the cause
of things, both of their essence and their existence: which
seems to have been noticed by those who have asserted that
God's intellect, will, and power are one and the same
thing. Now as God's intellect is the only cause of things,
i.e., the cause both of their essence and of their existence, it
must therefore necessarily differ from them in respect to
its essence and in respect to its existence. For that which
is caused differs from its cause precisely in that which it
has from its cause. For example, a man is the cause of the
existence but not the cause of the essence of another man
(for the latter is an eternal truth) and so they can certainly agree in essence, but in existence they must differ, and
on that account if the existence of one of them perish, that
of the other does not consequently perish; but if the essence of one of them could be destroyed or be made false,
the essence of the other must also be destroyed. On this account a thing that is the cause of the essence and existence
of any effect must differ from that effect both in respect to
its essence and in respect to its existence. Now the intellect of God is the cause of the essence and existence of

our intellect: and therefore God's intellect, in so far as it can be conceived to form part of his essence, differs from our intellect both in respect to its essence and in respect to its existence, nor in any other thing save name can agree with it, which we wished to prove. And the argument concerning will would proceed in the same manner, as can easily be seen.

XVIII. God is the immanent and not the transient cause of all things.

XIX. God is eternal. That is, all his attributes are eternal.

XX. God's existence and his essence are one and the same thing.

Corollary 1. Hence it follows that the existence of God, like his essence, is an eternal truth. . . .

XXI. All things which follow from the absolute nature of any attribute of God must exist forever and infinitely, that is, as eternal and infinite.

XXII. Whatever follows from an attribute of God, in so far as it is modified by such a modification as exists of necessity and infinitely through the same attributes, must also exist of necessity and infinitely.

XXIII. Every mode which of necessity and infinitely exists must of necessity follow either from the absolute nature of some attribute of God, or from some attribute modified by a modification which exists of necessity and infinitely.

XXIV. The essence of things produced by God does not involve existence.

Corollary. Hence it follows that God is not only the cause that all things begin to exist, but also that they continue to exist, or (to use a scholastic term) God is the cause of the being [*causa essendi*] of things. For when we consider the essence of things, either existing or non-existing, we find it to involve neither existence nor duration; so their essence cannot be the cause either of their existence or their duration, but only God, to whose nature alone existence appertains (Coroll. 1, Prop. 14).

XXV. God is not only the effecting cause of the existence of things, but also of their essence.

Corollary. Particular things are nothing else than affections of attributes of God, or modes by which attributes of God are expressed in a certain and determined manner. The proof of this is clear from Prop. 15 and Def. 5.

XXVI. A thing which is determined necessarily by God, and a thing which is not determined by God cannot determine of itself to do anything.

XXVII. A thing which is determined by God for the performing of anything cannot render itself undetermined.

Proof. This is obvious from the third axiom.

XXVIII. Every individual thing, or any thing that is finite and has a determined existence, cannot exist nor be determined for action unless it is determined for action and existence by another cause which is also finite and has a determined existence; and again, this cause also cannot exist nor be determined for action unless it be determined for existence and action by another cause which also is finite and has a determined existence: and so on to infinity. . . .

Note. As certain things must have been produced immediately by God, namely those things which necessarily follow from his absolute nature; those primary products being the mediating causes of other things, which nevertheless cannot exist nor be conceived without God, it follows that God is the proximate cause of those things immediately produced by him, absolutely, not, as some would have it, in his kind. For the effects of God cannot exist or be conceived without their cause (Prop. 15, and Coroll., Prop. 24). It follows, again, that God cannot be said in truth to be the remote cause of individual things unless we would thus distinguish these from the things which are immediately produced by God, or rather which follow from his absolute nature. For we understand by a remote cause one which is in no wise connected with its effect. But all things which are, are in God, and so depend on God that without him they can neither exist nor be conceived.

XXIX. In nature there is nothing contingent but all things are determined by the necessity of divine nature to exist and act in a certain way.

Note. Before proceeding, I would wish to explain, or rather to remind you, what we must understand by active and passive nature [*natura naturans* and *natura naturata*], for I think that from the past propositions it is agreed that by active nature we must understand that which is in itself and is conceived through itself, or such attributes of substance as express eternal and infinite essence, that is (Coroll. 1, Prop. 14, and Coroll. 2, Prop. 17), God, in so far as he is considered as a free cause. But by nature passive I understand all that follows from the necessity of the nature of God, or of any one of his attributes, that is, all the modes of the attributes of God, in so far as they are considered as things which are in God, and which cannot exist or be conceived without God.

XXX. Intellect, finite or infinite in actuality [*actus*], must comprehend the attributes of God and the affections of God and nothing else.

XXXI. The intellect in actuality, whether it be finite or infinite, together with will, desire, love, etc., must be referred not to active, but passive nature.

XXXII. Will can only be called a necessary cause, not a free one.

Corollary 1. Hence it follows that God does not act from freedom of will.

XXXIII. Things could not have been produced by God in any other manner or order than that in which they were produced.

Note 1. Although I have shown more clearly than the sun at noonday that there is absolutely nothing in things in virtue of which we can call them contingent, yet I would wish to explain here in a few words what is the signification of contingent; but first that of necessary and impossible. A thing is said to be necessary either by reason of its essence or its cause. For the existence of a thing necessarily follows either from its very essence or definition, or from a given effecting cause. A thing is said to be impossible for similar reasons: either because its essence or definition involves a contradiction, or because there is no external cause determined for the production of such a thing. But a thing cannot be called contingent save in respect to the imperfection of our knowledge. For when we are not aware that the essence of a thing involves a contradiction, or when we are quite certain that it does not involve a contradiction, and yet can affirm nothing with certainty concerning its existence, as the order of causes is hidden from us, such a thing can seem neither necessary or impossible to us: and therefore we call it either contingent or possible.

Note 2. It clearly follows from the preceding remarks that things were produced in consummate perfection by God, since they followed necessarily from an existing most perfect nature. Nor does this argue any imperfection in God, for his perfection has forced us to assert this. And from the contrary of this proposition it would have followed (as I have just shown) that God was not consummately perfect, inasmuch as if things were produced in any other way there must have been attributed to God a nature different to that which we are forced to attribute to him from the consideration of a perfect being. I make no doubt, however, that many will dismiss this opinion as absurd, nor will they agree to give up their minds to the contemplation of it and on no other account than that they are wont to ascribe to God a freedom far different to that which has been propounded by us (Def. 6). They attribute to him absolute will. Yet I make no doubt but that, if they would rightly consider the matter and follow our series of propositions, weighing well each of them, they would reject that freedom which they now attribute to God, not only as futile, but also clearly as an obstacle to knowledge. Nor is there any need for me here to repeat what was said in the note on Prop. 17. But for their benefit I shall show this much, that although it be conceded that will appertains to the essence of God, yet it nevertheless follows that things could not have been created in any other manner or order than that in which they were created; and this will be easy to show if first we consider the very thing which they themselves grant, namely, that it depends solely on the decree and will of God that each thing is what it is, for otherwise God would not be the cause of all things. They grant further that all the decrees of God have been appointed by him through and from all eternity: for otherwise it would argue mutability and imperfection in God. But as in eternity there are no such things as when, before, or after, it follows merely from the perfection of God that he never can or could decree anything else than what is decreed, that is, that God did not exist before his decrees, nor could exist without them. But they say that even if we suppose that God had made nature different or had decreed otherwise concerning nature and her order from all eternity, it would not thence follow that God was imperfect. Now if they say this, they must also admit that God can change his decrees. For had God decreed otherwise than he has concerning nature and her order, that is, had he willed and conceived anything else concerning nature, he would necessarily have had some other intellect and will than those which he now has. And if it is permitted to attribute to God another will and intellect than those which he now has, without any change in his essence or perfection, why should he not be able, even as it is, to change his decrees concerning things created, and yet remain perfect? For his intellect and will concerning things created and their order is the same in respect to his essence and perfection, however his intellect and will may be conceived. Furthermore, all the philosophers I have seen concede that there is no such thing as potential intellect in God, but only actual. But as they make no distinction between his intellect and will and his essence, being all agreed in this, it follows then that if God had another actual intellect and will, he must necessarily also have another essence; and thence, as I concluded in the beginning, that, were things produced in any other way than that in which they now exist, God's intellect and will, that is, as has been granted, his essence, also must have been other than they are, which is absurd.

Now since things could not have been produced in any other manner or order than that in which they were produced, and since this follows from the consummate perfection of God, there is no rational argument to persuade us to believe that God did not wish to create all the things which are in his intellect, in the same perfection as that in which his intellect conceived them. But they will say that in things there is no such thing as perfection or imperfection, but that which causes us to call a thing perfect or imperfect, good or bad, depends solely on the will of God; and so, if

God had willed it, he could have brought to pass that what is now perfection might have been the greatest imperfection, and vice versa. But what else is this than openly to assert that God, who necessarily understands what he wishes, could bring to pass by his own will that he should understand things in a manner different from that in which he understands them? This (as I have just shown) is the height of absurdity. Wherefore I can turn their argument against them in the following manner. All things depend on the power of God. That things should be different from what they are would involve a change in the will of God, and the will of God cannot change (as we have most clearly shown from the perfection of God): therefore things could not be otherwise than as they are. I confess that the theory which subjects all things to the will of an indifferent God, and makes them dependent on his good will, is not so far from the truth as that which states that God acts in all things for the furthering of good. For these seem to place something beyond God which does not depend on God, and to which God looks in his actions as to an example, or strives after as an ultimate end. Now this is nothing else than subjecting God to fate, a greater absurdity than which it is difficult to assert of God, whom we have shown to be the first and only free cause of the essence of all things and their existence. Wherefore let me not waste more time in refuting such idle arguments.

XXXIV. The power of God is the same as his essence.

XXXV. Whatever we conceive to be in the power of God necessarily exists.

XXXVI. Nothing exists from whose nature some effect does not follow.

Appendix

In these propositions I have explained the nature and properties of God: that he necessarily exists: that he is one alone: that he exists and acts merely from the necessity of his nature: that he is the free cause of all things and in what manner: that all things are in God, and so depend upon him that without him they could neither exist nor be

conceived: and, finally, that all things were predetermined
by God, not through his free or good will, but through his
absolute nature or infinite power. I have endeavoured,
moreover, whenever occasion prompted, to remove prejudices which might impede the good understanding of my
propositions. Yet, as many prejudices still remain, which,
to a very large extent, have prevented and do prevent men
from embracing the concatenation of things in the manner
in which I have explained it, I have thought it worth while
to call these up for the scrutiny of reason. Now since the
prejudices that I am here undertaking to point out depend
upon this one point, that men commonly suppose that all
natural things act like themselves with an end in view, and
since they assert with assurance that God directs all things
to a certain end (for they say that God made all things for
man, and man that he might worship God), I shall therefore consider this one thing first, inquiring in the first place
why so many fall into this error, and why all are by nature
so prone to embrace it; then I shall show its falsity, and
finally, how these prejudices have arisen concerning good
and evil, virtue and sin, praise and blame, order and confusion, beauty and ugliness, and other things of this kind.
But this is not the place to deduce these things from the
nature of the human mind. It will suffice here for me to take
as a basis of argument what must be admitted by all: that
is, that all men are born ignorant of the causes of things,
and that all have a desire of acquiring what is useful; that
they are conscious, moreover, of this. From these premises
it follows then, in the first place, that men think themselves
free inasmuch as they are conscious of their volitions and
desires, and as they are ignorant of the causes by which they
are led to wish and desire, they do not even dream of the existence of these causes. It follows, in the second place, that
men do all things with an end in view, that is, for that which
is profitable, which they seek. Whence it comes to pass
that they always seek out only the final causes of what has
happened, and when they have divined these, they cease, for
clearly then they have no cause of further doubt. If they are
unable to learn these causes from someone, nothing remains
for them but to turn to themselves and reflect what could in-

duce them personally to bring about such a thing, and thus they necessarily estimate other natures by their own. Furthermore, as they find in themselves and outside themselves many things which aid them not a little in their quest of things useful to themselves, as, for example, eyes for seeing, teeth for mastication, vegetables and animals for food, the sun for giving light, the sea for breeding fish, they consider all natural things alike to be made for their use; and as they know that they found these things as they were, and did not make them themselves, they have cause for believing that some one else prepared these things for their use. Now having considered things as means, they cannot believe them to be self-created; but they must conclude from the means which they are wont to prepare for themselves, that there is some governor or governors of nature, endowed with human freedom, who take care of all things for them and make all things for their use. They must naturally form an estimate of the nature of these governors from their own, for they have no information about it: and hence they come to say that the Gods direct all things for the use of men, that men may be bound down to them and do them the highest honour. Whence it has come about that each individual has devised a different manner in his own mind for the worship of God, that God may love him above the rest and direct the whole of nature for the gratification of his blind cupidity and insatiable avarice. Thus this prejudice became a superstition, and fixed its roots deeply in the mind, and this was the reason why all diligently tried to understand and explain the final causes of all things. But while they have sought to show that nature does nothing in vain (that is, nothing which is not of use to man), they appear to have shown nothing else than that nature and the Gods are as mad as men. Behold now, I pray you, what this thing has become. Among so many conveniences of nature they were bound to find some inconveniences—storms, earthquakes, and diseases, etc.—and they said these happened by reason of the anger of the Gods aroused against men through some misdeed or some omission in worship; and although experience daily belied this, and showed with infinite examples that conveniences and their contraries happen promiscuously to the pious and impious, yet not even then did they turn from their inveterate prejudice. For it was easier for them to place this among other unknown things whose use they did not know, and thus retain their present and innate condition of ignorance, than to destroy the whole fabric of their philosophy and reconstruct it. So it came to pass that they stated with the greatest certainty that the judgments of God far surpassed human comprehension: and this by itself was enough to keep truth hidden from the human race through all eternity, had not mathematics, which deals not in the final causes, but in the essence and properties of forms, offered to men another standard of truth. And besides mathematics there are other causes (which need not be enumerated here) which enabled men to take notice of these general prejudices and to be led to the true knowledge of things.

Thus I have explained what I undertook in the first place. It is scarcely necessary that I should show that nature has no fixed aim in view, and that all final causes are merely fabrications of men. For I think this is sufficiently clear from the bases and causes from which I have traced the origin of this prejudice, from Prop. 16, and the corollaries of Prop. 32, and, above all, from all those propositions in which I have shown that all things are produced by a certain eternal necessity of nature and with the utmost perfection. Here, however, I shall pause to overthrow entirely that foolish doctrine of a final cause. For that which in truth is a cause it considers as an effect, and vice versa, and so it makes that which is first by nature to be last, and again, that which is highest and most perfect it renders imperfect. As these two questions are obvious, let us pass them over. It follows from Props. 21, 22 and 23 that the effect which is produced immediately from God is the most perfect, and that one is more imperfect according as it requires more intermediating causes. But if those things which are immediately produced by God are made by him for the attaining of some end, then it necessarily follows that the ultimate things for whose sake these first were made must transcend all others. Hence this doctrine destroys the perfection of God: for if God seeks an end, he necessarily de-

sires something which he lacks. And although theologians
and metaphysicians make a distinction between the end of
want and that of assimilation, they confess that God acts
on his own account, and not for the sake of creating things:
for before the creation they can assign nothing save God
on whose account God acted, and so necessarily they are
obliged to confess that God lacked and desired those things
for the attainment of which he wished to prepare means,
as is clear of itself. Nor must I omit at this point that
some of the adherents of this doctrine, who have wished to
show their ingenuity in assigning final causes to things,
have discovered a new manner of argument for the proving
of their doctrine, to wit, not a reduction to the impossible,
but a reduction to ignorance, which shows that they have
no other mode of arguing their doctrine. For example, if
a stone falls from a roof on the head of a passer-by and
kills him, they will show by their method of argument that
the stone was sent to fall and kill the man; for if it had not
fallen on him by God's will, how could so many circumstances (for often very many circumstances concur at the
same time) concur by chance? You will reply, perhaps:
"That the wind was blowing, and that the man had to pass
that way, and hence it happened." But they will retort:
"Why was the wind blowing at that time? and why was the
man going that way at that time?" If again you reply: "That
the wind had then arisen on account of the agitation of the
sea the day before, and the previous weather had been
calm, and that the man was going that way at the invitation of a friend," they will again retort, for there is no end
to their questioning: "Why was the sea agitated, and why
was the man invited at that time?" And thus they will pursue you from cause to cause until you are glad to take refuge
in the will of God, that is, the asylum of ignorance. Thus
again, when they see the human body they are amazed,
and as they do not know the cause of so much art, they conclude that it was made not by mechanical art, but divine
or supernatural art, and constructed in such a manner that
one part may not injure another. And hence it comes about
that those who wish to seek out the causes of miracles, and
who wish to understand the things of nature as learned men,

and not stare at them in amazement like fools, are soon deemed heretical and impious, and proclaimed such by those whom the mob adore as the interpreters of nature and the Gods. For these know that once ignorance is laid aside, that wonderment, on which alone they rely in argument and for the preservation of their authority, would be taken away from them. But I now leave this point and proceed to what I determined to discuss in the third place.

As soon as men had persuaded themselves that all things which were made, were made for their sakes, they were bound to consider as the best quality in everything that which was the most useful to them, and to esteem that above all things which brought them the most good. Hence they must have formed these notions by which they explain the things of nature, to wit, good, evil, order, confusion, hot, cold, beauty, and ugliness, etc.; and as they deemed themselves free agents, the notions of praise and blame, sin and merit, arose. The latter notions I will discuss when I deal with human nature later on, but the former I shall briefly explain here. They call all that which is conducive to health and the worship of God good, and all which is conducive to the contrary, evil. And forasmuch as those who do not understand the things of nature are certain of nothing concerning these things, but only imagine them and mistake their imagination for intellect, they firmly believe there is order in things, and are ignorant of them and their own nature. Now when things are so disposed that, when they are represented to us through our senses, we can easily imagine and consequently easily remember them, we call them well-ordered; and on the other hand, when we cannot do so, we call them ill-ordered or confused. Now forasmuch as those things, above all others, are pleasing to us which we can easily imagine, men accordingly prefer order to confusion, as if order were anything in nature save in respect to our imagination; and they say that God has created all things in order, and thus unwittingly they attribute imagination to God, unless indeed they mean that God, providing for human imagination, disposed all things in such a manner as would be most easy for our imagination; nor would they then find it perhaps a stumbling-block to their

theory that infinite things are found which are far beyond
the reach of our imagination, and many which confuse it
through its weakness. But of this I have said enough. The
other notions also are nothing other than modes of imagining in which the imagination is affected in diverse manners,
and yet they are considered by the ignorant as the chief
attributes of things: for, as we have said, they think all
things were made for them, and call the nature of a thing
good or bad, healthy, or rotten and corrupt, according as
they are affected by it. For example, if motion, which the
nerves receive by means of the eyes from the objects before
us, is conducive to health, those objects by which it is
caused are called beautiful; if it is not, then the objects are
called ugly. Such things as affect the nerves by means of the
nose are thus styled fragrant or evil-smelling; or when by
means of the mouth, sweet or bitter, tasty or insipid; when
by means of touch, hard or soft, rough or smooth, etc. And
such things as affect the ear are called noises, and form dis-
cord or harmony, the last of which has delighted men to
madness, so that they have believed that harmony delights
God. Nor have there been wanting philosophers who assert
that the movements of the heavenly spheres make up a harmony. All of which sufficiently shows that each man judges
concerning things according to the disposition of his own
mind, or rather takes for things what are really affections of
his imagination. Wherefore it is not remarkable (as we may
incidentally remark) that so many controversies as we find
have arisen among men, and at last Scepticism. For although
human bodies agree in many points, yet in many others they
differ, and that which seems to one good may yet to another seem evil; to one order, yet to another confusion; to
one pleasing, yet to another displeasing, and so on, for I
need not treat further of these, as this is not the place to
discuss them in detail, and indeed they must be sufficiently
obvious to all. For it is in every one's mouth: "As many
minds as men," "Each is wise in his own manner," "As
tastes differ, so do minds"—all of which proverbs show
clearly enough that men judge things according to the disposition of their minds, and had rather imagine things than
understand them. For if they understood things, my argu-

ment would convince them at least, just as mathematics does, although they might not attract them.

We have thus seen that all the arguments by which the vulgar are wont to explain nature are nothing else than modes of imagination, and indicate the nature of nothing whatever, but only the constitution of the imagination; and although they have names as if they were entities existing outside the imagination, I call them entities, not of reality, but of the imagination; and so all arguments directed against us from such notions can easily be rebutted. For many are wont to argue thus: If all things have followed from the necessity of the most perfect nature of God, whence have so many imperfections in nature arisen? For example, the corruption of things till they stink, the ugliness of things which often nauseate, confusion, evil, sin, etc. But as I have just said, these are easily confuted. For the perfection of things is estimated solely from their nature and power; nor are things more or less perfect according as they delight or disgust human senses, or according as they are useful or useless to men. But to those who ask, "Why did not God create all men in such a manner that they might be governed by reason alone?" I make no answer but this: because material was not wanting to him for the creating of all things from the highest grade to the lowest; or speaking more accurately, because the laws of his nature were so comprehensive as to suffice for the creation of everything that infinite intellect can conceive, as I have shown in Prop. 16. These are the misunderstandings which I stopped here to point out. If any grains of them still remain, they can be easily dispersed by means of a little reflection.]

IN BOOK II OF THE *Ethics* SPINOZA CONSIDERS THE NATURE of the human mind. His argument hinges on his concept of "an idea," inherited from Descartes, but adapted. Already in Axiom 6 of Book I, he had stated that an idea is true in so far as it agrees with that of which it is the idea. Here (Definition 4) he defines "adequate idea" as that which has all the *intrinsic* marks of a true idea. Spinoza pictures the progress of the human mind to higher levels of knowledge as a substitution of adequate ideas for inadequate ones. This progress each man can begin for himself, but, being a finite mode, he can never complete it. The ideal of knowledge is knowledge of self-evidently true ideas which represent the relation between essences, and he holds that there is no real knowledge which does not show itself as indubitable and self-evident. Below this level there are two stages: reasoning, or inference, and, below that, mere common opinion about matters of fact and imagination. These three levels he illustrates with an example in Proposition 40, Note 2. In an earlier work, *The Treatise on the Correction of the Understanding,* in a passage which is given at the end of these extracts, he distinguishes four levels, dividing the lowest level into two. Spinoza's use of "idea" and "object of an idea" is peculiar to himself and is the kernel of his argument.

The human mind itself is an idea, and its object is the human body. Here it must be remembered that thought and extension are only attributes under which the one substance is conceived. Thus, the same event can, for Spinoza, be considered as something happening both in the sphere of thought, to a person's mind, and to his body. The thoughts are inseparable from happenings in the body. This is not, however Leibniz's "pre-established Harmony" of Soul and Body, where two sets of events are happily made coincident by God; for Spinoza, they are the same event looked at from different aspects. In sense perception and ordinary experience, the mind has only confused and inadequate ideas, reflecting what happens in the body. Such ideas do not bear the internal marks of adequacy (Proposition 29 and Corollary). Our knowledge of individual existents outside us is only obtained through affections of the body by external objects, and it is for this reason that sense perception can give us only confused and inadequate ideas. These last points are the parallel within the theory of knowledge of Spinoza's metaphysical doctrine that the chain of causes of particular things can never be brought to a conclusion, and that therefore they can never be directly deduced from the nature of God or reality as a whole. (See also the extract from the *Correction of the Understanding.*)

But we are not confined to such inadequate ideas, which

are the products of the "imagination." We all necessarily possess also some knowledge of the second and third order, some reason and intuition of self-evident truths. This is how we are able to distinguish the true from the false; for we each possess a model of the truth, since we each know some necessary truths about the Universe as a whole. These are the common notions—e.g., that everything has a cause—on which all our reasoning is founded. The path from bondage to freedom can be followed by each one of us if he sets himself to build up on the foundation of common notions a view of the Universe as a whole, including his own place in it. It is the purpose of the *Ethics* to point the way to this path.

Here, in accordance with the design of this book, the extracts from Spinoza must be concluded. But it must never be forgotten that Spinoza's metaphysics is designed as a background for his *Ethics*. He has explained how the mind, in so far as it remains at the ordinary level of empirical knowledge, is passive and affected mainly by things outside itself. In the third book he applies this distinction between pure thought, which is active, and perception and ordinary opinion, which are passive, to the life of feeling. He gives a theory of the emotions which represents them as passive ideas reflecting modifications of the body produced by external objects. At the highest level of knowledge, where the mind moves solely among eternal truths, applicable to the universe as a whole, we are free from the influence of particular things around us. Spinoza denies free will in the common sense. But the mind can set itself free, nevertheless, by its own efforts, and, in enjoyment of pure thought, become for a time occupied with eternal truths. From such understanding happiness and freedom will result; not in the sense of a stoical resignation to fate, but in the sense that the mind is free from particular interests, and the emotions which these engender, and is interested only in the unchanging features of the universe. This constitutes the love of God and of Nature.

Spinoza's whole manner of argument in the *Ethics* is open to the criticism which Hume and Kant were to bring later. He seeks to deduce from the nature of things what must be the highest type of life. Hume and Kant have shown that such a procedure cannot be defended in logic. Other critics have remarked that his arguments are less rigorous than they are made to appear; for the geometrical method does not in fact provide a series of strictly deductive proofs, and it could not be expected to do so. He is a philosopher whom people have tended generally either to revere or to revile, in both cases commonly without understanding his intentions. But he did not expect either his own works, or the manner of life he advocated, to be easy. As he says in the note to the last proposition of the last book *"omnia praeclara tam difficilia quam rara sunt"* ("All excellent things are as difficult as they are rare"). He is not a mystic, but a rationalist who makes greater claims for the powers of pure reason than any other great philosopher has ever made.

[Part II. *Concerning the Nature and Origin of the Mind. Preface.*

I now pass on to explain such things as must follow from the essence of God or of a being eternal and infinite: not all of them indeed (for they must follow in infinite number and infinite ways, as we have shown in Part I, Prop. 16), but only such as can lead us by the hand (so to speak) to the knowledge of the human mind and its consummate blessedness.

Definitions

I. By Body [*corpus*] I understand that mode which expresses in a certain determined manner the essence of God in so far as he is considered as an extended thing (*vide* Part I, Prop. 25, Coroll.).

II. I say that appertains to the essence of a thing which, when granted, necessarily involves the granting of the thing, and which, when removed, necessarily involves the removal of the thing; or that without which the thing can neither exist nor be conceived, and which, conversely, can neither exist nor be conceived without the thing.

III. By Idea I understand a conception of the mind which the mind forms by reason of its being a thinking thing.

Explanation. I say conception rather than perception, for the word perception seems to indicate that the mind is passive in relation to the object, while conception seems to express an action of the mind.

IV. By an Adequate Idea I understand an idea which in so far as it is considered with respect to the object, has all the properties or intrinsic marks of a true idea.

Explanation. I say intrinsic in order to exclude what is extrinsic, i.e., the agreement between the idea and its object. (See Book I, Ax. 6.)

V. Duration is indefinite continuation of existing.

Explanation. I say indefinite, because it can in no wise be determined by means of the nature itself of an existing thing nor by the efficient cause, which necessarily imposes existence on a thing but does not take it away.

VI. Reality and Perfection I understand to be one and the same thing.

VII. By Individual Things I understand things which are finite and have a determined existence; but if several of them so concur in one action that they all are at the same time the cause of one effect, I consider them all thus far as one individual thing.

Axioms

I. The essence of man does not involve necessary existence, that is, in the order of nature it can as well happen that this or that man exists as that he does not exist.

II. Man thinks.

III. The modes of thinking, such as love, desire, or any other name by which the affections of the mind are designated, do not exist unless there is an idea in the same individual of the thing loved, desired, etc. But the idea can exist although no other mode of thinking exists.

IV. We feel that a certain body is affected in many ways.

V. We neither feel nor perceive any individual things save bodies and modes of thinking.

Propositions

I. Thought is an attribute of God, or God is a thinking thing.

II. Extension is an attribute of God, or God is an extended thing.

VII. The order and connection of ideas is the same as the order and connection of things.

XI. The first thing that constitutes the actual being of the human mind is nothing else than the idea of an individual thing actually existing.

XII. Whatever happens in the object of the idea constituting the human mind must be perceived by the human mind; in other words the idea of that thing must necessarily be found in the human mind: that is, if the object of the idea constituting the human mind be a body, nothing can happen in that body which is not perceived by the mind.

XIII. The object of the idea constituting the human mind is a body, or a certain mode of extension actually existing and nothing else.

Note. Hence we understand not only that the human mind is united to the body, but also what must be understood by the union of the mind and body. But in truth no one will be able to understand this adequately or distinctly unless, at first, he is sufficiently acquainted with the nature of our body. For those things which we have so far propounded have been altogether general, and have not referred more to man than to the other individual things which are all, though in various grades, animate [*animata*]. For of all things there must necessarily be granted an idea in God, of which idea God is the cause, just as he is of the idea of the human body; and so whatever we say concerning the idea of the human body must necessarily be said concerning the idea of any other thing. Nevertheless we cannot deny that, like objects, ideas differ one from another, one transcending the others and having more reality, according as the object of one idea transcends the object of another or

contains more reality than it. And so for the sake of determining in what the human mind differs from other things,
and in what it excels other things. we must know the nature
of its object, as we have said, that is, the human body. What
this nature is, I am unable to explain here. but that is not
necessary for what I am going to show. This, however. I will
say in general. that according as one body is more adapted
than others for doing and suffering many things at the same
time. so is one mind more adapted than others for perceiving many things at the same time: and the more the actions
of a body depend solely on itself. and the fewer other bodies
concur with its action, so the mind is more apt for distinct
understanding And thus we may recognise how one mind
is superior to all others. and likewise see the cause why
we have only a very confused knowledge of our body, and
many other things which I shall deduce from these.

XXVI The human mind perceives no external body as
actually existing save through ideas of affections of its body.

XXVII The ideas of the affections of the human body,
in so far as they are referred to the human mind alone, are
not clear and distinct but confused.

XXIX The idea of the idea of each affection of the
human mind does not involve an adequate knowledge of
the human mind.

Corollary Hence it follows that the human mind, whenever it perceives a thing in the common order of nature,
has no adequate knowledge of itself. nor of its body nor of
external bodies but only a confused and mutilated knowledge thereof. For the mind does not know itself save in so
far as it perceives ideas of affections of the body (Prop. 23,
Part II) But it does not perceive its body save through the
ideas of affections. through which also it only perceives
external bodies (Props 23 and 26. Part II) And therefore
in so far as it has these ideas. it has no adequate knowledge
of itself (Prop. 29, Part II), nor of its body (Prop 27,
Part II). nor of external bodies (Prop. 25, Part II), but
only (Prop. 28 and Note, Part II) a confused and mutilated one. Q.E.D.

Note. I say expressly that the mind has no adequate but
only confused knowledge of itself, of its body, and of ex-

ternal bodies, when it perceives a thing in the common order of nature, that is, whenever it is determined externally, that is, by fortuitous circumstances, to contemplate this or that, and not when it is determined internally, that is, by the fact that it regards many things at once, to understand their agreements, differences, and oppositions one to another. For whenever it is disposed in this or any other way from within, then it regards things clearly and distinctly, as I shall show further on.

XXXI. We can only have a very inadequate knowledge about the duration of individual things outside us.

XXXV. Falsity consists in privation of knowledge which is involved by inadequate or mutilated and confused ideas.

XXXVI. Inadequate and confused ideas follow from the same necessity as adequate or clear and distinct ideas.

XXXVII. Those things which are common to everything, and which are equally in a part and in the whole, can only be conceived as adequate.

XXXIX. That which is common to, and a property of, the human body and certain external bodies by which the human body is affected, and which is equally in the part and whole of these, has an adequate idea in the mind. . . .

Note 2. From all that has been said above it is now clearly apparent that we perceive many things and form universal notions, first, from individual things represented to our intellect in a mutilated, confused, and random manner (Coroll., Prop. 29, Part II), and therefore I am wont to call such perceptions knowledge from vague or casual experience [*cognitio ab experientia vaga*]; second, from signs, e.g., from the fact that we remember certain things through having read or heard certain words and form certain ideas of them similar to those through which we imagine things (Note, Prop. 18, Part II). Both of these ways of regarding things I shall call hereafter knowledge of the first kind, opinion [*opinio*], or imagination [*imaginatio*]. Third, from the fact that we have common notions and adequate ideas of the properties of things (Coroll., Prop. 38, Coroll. and Prop. 39, and Prop. 40, Part II). And I shall call this reason [*ratio*] and knowledge of the second kind. Besides

these two kinds of knowledge there is a third, as I shall show
in what follows, which we call intuition [*scientia intuitiva*],
Now this kind of knowing proceeds from an adequate idea
of the formal essence of certain attributes of God to the
adequate knowledge of the essence of things. I shall illustrate these three by one example. Let three numbers be
given to find the fourth, which is in the same proportion
to the third as the second is to the first. Tradesmen without
hesitation multiply the second by the third and divide the
product by the first: either because they have not forgotten the rule which they received from the schoolmaster
without any proof, or because they have often found it with
very small numbers, or by conviction of the proof of Prop.
19, Book VII, of Euclid's elements, namely, the common
property of proportionals. But with very small numbers
there is no need of this, for when the numbers 1, 2, 3, are
given, who is there who could not see that the fourth proportional is 6? And this is much clearer because we conclude the fourth number from the same ratio which intuitively we see the first bears to the second.

XLI. Knowledge of the first kind is the only cause of
falsity; knowledge of the second and third kinds is necessarily true.

XLII. Knowledge of the second and third kinds, and not
of the first kind, teaches us to distinguish the true from
the false.

XLIII. He who has a true idea, knows at that same time
that he has a true idea, nor can he doubt concerning the
truth of the thing.

XLIV. It is not the nature of reason to regard things
as contingent, but as necessary.

Corollary 1. Hence it follows that it depends solely on
the imagination that we consider things, whether in respect
to the past or future, as contingent.

Corollary 2. It is the nature of reason to perceive things
under a certain form of eternity [*sub quadam aeternitatis
specie*].

XLV. Every idea of every body or individual thing actually existing necessarily involves the eternal and infinite
essence of God.

XLVI. The knowledge of the eternal and infinite essence of God which each idea involves is adequate and perfect.

XLVII The human mind has an adequate knowledge of the eternal and infinite essence of God.

XLVIII There is in no mind absolute or free will, but the mind is determined for willing this or that by a cause which is determined in its turn by another cause, and this one again by another, and so on to infinity.

On the Correction of the Understanding

I may now turn my attention to what is the most important subject of all, namely, to the correction of the understanding and to the means of making it able to understand things in such a way as is necessary to the attainment of our end. To bring this about, the natural order we observe demands that I should recapitulate all the modes of perception which I have used thus far for the indubitable affirmation or negation of anything so that I may choose the best of all, and at the same time begin to know my powers and nature which I wish to perfect.

19. If I remember rightly, they can all be reduced to four headings. namely ——

I. Perception which we have *by hearsay* or from some sign, which may be called to suit any one's taste.

II. Perception which we have *from vague experience*, that is. from experience which is not determined by the intellect but is only so called because it happened by chance and we have no experienced fact to oppose to it, and so it remain unchallenged in our minds.

III. Perception *wherein the essence of one thing is concluded from the essence of another*, but not adequately: this happens when we infer a cause from some effect, or when it is concluded from some general notion that it is accompanied always by some property.

IV. Finally, perception *wherein a thing is perceived through its essence alone* or through a knowledge of its proximate cause.

20. All these I shall illustrate by examples. *By hearsay*

alone I know my birthday, and that certain people were
my parents, and the like: things of which I have never had
any doubt. *By vague experience* I know that I shall die; and
I assert that inasmuch as I have seen men like me undergo
death, although they did not all live for the same space of
time, nor died of the same illness. Again, *by vague experience* I know also that oil is good for feeding a flame, that
water is good for extinguishing it. I know also that a dog
is a barking animal, and man a rational animal: and in this
way I know nearly all things that are useful in life. 21.
We conclude one thing *from another* in the following manner: After we have clearly perceived that we feel a certain
body and no other, we thence conclude clearly that a soul
or mind is united to that body, and that the union is the
cause of that feeling; but what is this feeling and union we
cannot absolutely understand from that. Or after I know
the nature of vision, and that it has such a property that we
see a thing smaller when at a great distance than when we
look at it close, I can conclude that the sun is larger than
it appears, and other similar things.

22. Finally, a thing is said to be perceived *through its
essence alone* when from the fact that I know something,
I know what it is to know anything, or from the fact that
I know the essence of the mind, I know it to be united to the
body. By the same knowledge we know that two and three
make five, and that if there are two lines parallel to the
same line they are parallel to each other, etc. But the
things which I have been able to know by this knowledge
so far have been very few.

23. In order that all these things may be better understood I shall employ just one example, namely this: Three
numbers are given to find the fourth, which is to the third
as the second is to the first. Tradesmen will say at once that
they know what is to be done to find the fourth number,
inasmuch as they have not yet forgotten the operation,
which they learned without proof from their teachers.
Others again, from experimenting with small numbers
where the fourth number is quite manifest, as with 2, 4, 3,
and 6, where it is found that by multiplying the second by
the third and dividing the answer by the first number, the

quotient is six, have made it an axiom, and when they find
this number which, without that working out, they knew
to be the proportional, they thence conclude that this
process is good invariably for finding the fourth proportional.

24. But mathematicians, by conviction of the proof of
Prop. 19, Bk. VII, *Elements* of Euclid, know what numbers
are proportionals from the nature and property of proportion, namely, that the first and fourth multiplied together
are equal to the product of the second and third. But they
do not see the adequate proportionality of the given numbers; if they do, it is not on the strength of that proposition, but intuitively without any process of working out.

XIV. *Of the Means by which Eternal Things are known*

. . . We can see that it is above all things necessary to us that we should deduce all our ideas from physical things or from real entities, proceeding, as far as
possible, according to the series of causes from one real
entity to another, and in such a manner that we never pass
over to generalities and abstractions, either in order to
conclude anything real from them or to deduce them from
anything real; for either of these interrupts the true progress of the intellect.

100. But it must be noted that I do not understand here
by that series of causes and real entities a series of individual mutable things, but only the series of fixed and
eternal things. For it would be impossible for human weakness to follow up the series of individual mutable things,
both on account of their number exceeding all count, and
on account of the many circumstances in one and the same
thing of which each one may be the cause that it exists
or does not. For indeed their existence has no connection
with their essence, or (as I have said) it is not an eternal
truth.

101. However, there is no need that we should understand this series, for the essences of individual mutable
things are not to be drawn from the series or order of
existence, which would afford us nothing save their ex-

trinsic denominations, relations, or at the most their circumstances, which are far removed from the inmost essence of things. But this is only to be sought from fixed and
eternal things, and from the laws inscribed in those things
as in their true codes, according to which all individual
things are made and arranged: nay, these individual and
mutable things depend so intimately and essentially (so
to speak) on these fixed ones that without them they can
neither exist nor be conceived. Whence these fixed and
eternal things, although they are individual, yet on account
of their presence everywhere and their widespread power,
will be to us like generalities or kinds of definitions of individual mutable things, and the proximate causes of all
things.

102. But although this be so, there seems to be no small
difficulty to surmount in order that we may arrive at the
knowledge of the individual things, for to conceive all things
at once is a thing far beyond the power of human understanding. For one thing to be understood before another,
however, the order, as we said, is not to be looked for from
the series of existence, nor even from eternal things; for
with these things all are simultaneous in nature. Whence
other aids must necessarily be sought beside those which
we employed to understand eternal things and their laws.]

CHAPTER VII

Leibniz

GOTTFRIED WILHELM VON LEIBNIZ WAS BORN AT LEIPZIG
in 1646 and died in 1716. His father died when he was six,
his mother when he was eighteen. He was a prodigy of
learning and precocity as a young man, and described himself later as an "autodidact." He studied law, and at the
age of twenty published an important treatise (*Ars Com-
binatoria*) which anticipated later discoveries in logic and
mathematics and showed the foundations of his new philosophy. Germany at this time was still recovering from the
horrors and divisions of the Thirty Years' War, still back-
ward and chaotic, its intellectual life often centering round
secret societies of alchemists and Rosicrucians and the
remnants of Renaissance magic. Leibniz was then in con-
tact with these secret societies, but soon found his way
to the courts of Frankfurt and Mainz, where he codified
laws and drafted schemes for the unification of the churches.
He remained all his life a versatile courtier, civil servant
and international lawyer, vastly prolific in learned and in-
genious defenses of any case, religious or secular, which
he was required to defend. At the same time he studied
and assimilated the science, philosophy and mathematics
of his time, particularly the work of Galileo, Descartes,
Pascal, and Boyle. He entered into relations with the Royal
Society in London and the Académie des Sciences in Paris;
and he addressed works on physical theory to those societies. In 1672 he went first to Paris, on a diplomatic
mission, and then to London, where he met Oldenburg,
secretary of the Royal Society, the great chemist Boyle,
and Christopher Wren. In 1676 he visited Spinoza at The
Hague, and arrived at Hanover to take up his post as li-

brarian to the Duke of Brunswick. He had already formulated the principle of the differential and integral calculus. The main outlines of his natural philosophy seem already to have been fixed in his mind. In addition to his work for the Dukes of Brunswick, he maintained a vast learned correspondence and elaborated, without publishing, his own mathematical and philosophical discoveries. In 1684 and 1685 the first of his essays on infinitesimals, and on knowledge and truth, appeared. After traveling through Vienna to Italy in the years 1687 to 1690, he returned to Hanover to find himself overwhelmed by the history of the House of Brunswick which he had undertaken to write, and by an astonishing variety of other projects, legal, scholarly, mathematical and philosophical. In 1700 he went to Berlin to found the Prussian Academy of the Sciences, and later he entered into relations with the Tsar with a view to founding an academy in Russia. In 1714 he fell ill in Vienna, and returned to Hanover to find that the Elector had left for London to become king of England. At this time began the celebrated controversy with the friends of Newton in England, who claimed that Leibniz had plagiarized the idea of the calculus, and that the credit for the discovery should go to Newton. In 1716, still with the great bulk of his mathematical and philosophical work unpublished, he died in Hanover. Only the *Theodicy,* subtitled "Essays on the Goodness of God, the Freedom of Man and the Origin of Evil," had been published, anonymously, in 1710.

Leibniz was perhaps the most universal genius of the modern world, comparable in insight with Newton, wider in range and lesser only in ultimate achievement. He rightly said of himself: "He who knows me only from published works, does not know me." He wrote many hundreds of treatises and fragments, touching on almost every branch of modern knowledge. Even now the whole of his work has not been published. He was the last man who could hope to master the whole range of modern knowledge, and to be an encyclopedia in himself. He was a visionary optimist, with an unlimited faith in reason and enlightenment, who prepared schemes for the reunion of the churches and for European peace, foresaw and designed in outline a new science of statistics, contributed to the theory of probability, was a founder of symbolic logic, projected a universal language, studied optics, conceived the idea of calculating machines, speculated on human history, organized scientific research, and foresaw a new age of invention in mechanics His thought, and his vision of great academies of knowledge and enlightenment, was the foundation of eighteenth-century rationalism.

His philosophical system – and it is a tightly knit system—is scattered in different, and often occasional, works. The more complete statements are to be found in the *Discourse on Metaphysics*, in the *New Essays on the Understanding*, the *Monadology*, and in the *Letters* (to Samuel Clarke) *on Newton's Mathematical Principles of Philosophy*. The following extracts are taken also from some shorter essays and letters.

Leibniz distinguished two types of statements—those which state necessary truth, established as true by reference to the principle of non-contradiction alone, and contingent statements, which cannot be established to be true solely by reference to the principle of non-contradiction. This distinction is the center of Leibniz's philosophy. Necessary propositions define the limit of what is logically possible: but not everything which is logically possible is actual, and contingent propositions state which of the various possible arrangements of things is actually realized and exists. It is certain that a benevolent God exists, and since we know that he is benevolent and all-powerful, we know that he must have chosen the best of all the logically possible worlds. Therefore, in science, we must always, when we are concerned with the truth of contingent statements, prefer that hypothesis which shows the greatest possible number of effects as deducible from the smallest number of causes; that is, in judging of the truth of contingent statements, we must use the principle that God had a sufficient reason for creating things as he did. In this principle—which may be interpreted as the demand for simplicity in explanation—Leibniz thought that he had found a general method of discovery in science. He proposed a new and closer relationship between the different sciences, which he thought would everywhere illustrate a few simple and general principles of order. In the domain of necessary truths, Leibniz realized that there could be no essential distinction between logic and mathematics, and he looked forward to the possibility of a uniform and clear notation, in which any necessary truth could be established by mere calculation or the mechanical manipulation of symbols; to this end he proposed a universal logistic or calculus, anticipating, at least in outline, the work of Bertrand Russell and of symbolic logicians in this century. An extract is given below.

Closely following these doctrines of logic, Leibniz argued that the universe, created by the free and beneficent choice of God, must be conceived as consisting, in the last analysis, of ultimate substances, called Monads, each of which contains in itself all the attributes which can be truly predicated of it. Consequently there can be no interaction between these substances, and the monads must be, in Leibniz's phrase, "windowless." This theory of monads is the metaphysical counterpart of the logical doctrine that in any true judgment of the subject-predicate form, the predicate must be contained in the subject. All the attributes of a substance are necessarily connected, and, if our human minds were capable of carrying through an infinite analysis, we would be able to show that all true subject-predicate propositions are necessarily true. The only propositions which are not necessarily true in the last resort, even for God, are those which state that there exists a substance possessing such-and-such an attribute. But given that there exists a substance possessing a particular attribute, it is possible, in principle though not in practice, to deduce all the other attributes of the substance from the given one. From these principles it follows also that no two substances can have all their attributes in common—Leibniz's celebrated principle of the Identity of Indiscernibles; for a substance cannot be distinguished from the set of its properties.

Leibniz's system defines with unusual clarity the basic notions which must be related to each other in any systematic philosophy–Identity, Subject and Attribute, Necessity and Contingency, Existence, Truth and Knowledge. He adjusts his account of these organizing concepts in such a way as to allow a place for a benevolent God who has freely created a world which is entirely intelligible. The world which God has created must exhibit a few universal principles of order, which ought to guide us in framing hypotheses to explain phenomena; for we have in metaphysics an assurance that the actual world is the most rationally ordered of all possible worlds.

His arguments are of some complexity and are intended to fit tightly. Some, but not all, of the main difficulties of interpretation are mentioned below.

The first extract stands on its own, the formulation of the project which Leibniz conceived early in his life, and never carried out, although various scraps of work for it survive. The project of a "universal character," which would eliminate difficulties of ambiguity in one language, and of translation between several, by providing a general symbolism based on simple ideas, was widely discussed in the seventeenth and eighteenth centuries.

Leibniz's conception of such a language, to be modeled on the symbolism of arithmetic or geometry, has been noted as a forerunner of the systems of symbolic logic which, beginning with Boole and Schröder in the nineteenth century, were developed by Frege, Russell and Whitehead and others, and are widely employed and discussed today. Such systems have in fact proved of most value in the study of the logical foundation of mathematics itself; it is only in a few corners of the sciences that their application has been attempted.

Leibniz shows both far-sightedness and some caution in his formulation of the idea. The famous remark of "calculemus ("let us calculate") is a forerunner of that eighteenth-century optimism which hoped, in the phrase of Condorcet, to carry "les flambeaux de l'algèbre" into the darkest corners of human thought; yet his qualification "in so far as they are amenable to reasoning" leaves open the question of what subject matter we may be able to cast into the formalized language.

[*On Method.* Preface to the General Science (1677)

It is manifest that if we could find characters or signs appropriate to the expression of all our thoughts as definitely and as exactly as numbers are expressed by arithmetic or lines by geometrical analysis, we could in all subjects, in so far as they are amenable to reasoning, accomplish what is done in Arithmetic and Geometry.

All inquiries which depend on reasoning would be performed by the transposition of characters and by a kind of calculus which would directly assist the discovery of elegant results. We should not have to puzzle our heads as much as we have to-day, and yet we should be sure of accomplishing everything the given facts allowed.

Moreover, we should be able to convince the world of what we had discovered or inferred, since it would be easy to verify the calculation either by doing it again or by trying tests similar to that of casting out nines in arithmetic. And if someone doubted my results, I should say to him "Let us calculate, Sir," and so by taking pen and ink we should soon settle the question.]

THE PHILOSOPHY OF LEIBNIZ, TO A GREATER EXTENT THAN any other, can be seen as following from a few simple axioms; and Leibniz himself did not fail to single these out, emphasize them, name them, and often incorporate them in some telling phrase. Another great merit of his system is that his metaphysics is connected integrally and naturally with his logic; his view of the world as consisting of "windowless monads," and his theory of free will, are both based firmly on his logical doctrines about predication, and necessity and contingency, and on the law of sufficient reason. These basic logical notions are what will principally concern us in the first set of extracts.

1. *Subject, Predicate and Substance.* We may start with the law of non-contradiction; this is merely the requirement that a proposition and its opposite cannot both be true—and that any proposition which implies a contradiction, or contains elements that implicitly deny each other, is false, and, indeed, absurd. Leibniz is able, using this principle, to

distinguish what he calls "truths of reason" and "truths of fact" and, correspondingly, the concepts of necessity and contingency. A truth of reason is a proposition which is "true in virtue of the law of non-contradiction alone"; that is, its *denial* implies a contradiction. Such propositions are necessarily true. Truths of fact, on the other hand, are propositions which are indeed true, but not *necessarily* so, in the strong sense of "logical necessity"; their denial does not imply a contradiction, and so is possible and conceivable. Truths of fact are only *contingently* true. Kant (himself in his earlier years a Leibnizian) gave the terms "analytic" and "synthetic" respectively to these two types of proposition; and under these terms the distinction remains of great importance in philosophy today.

The terms "analytic" and "synthetic," which were not employed by Leibniz himself, do in fact imply his own way of presenting the distinctions: even though radically different types of proposition were attached to either side of the division by Leibniz and by Kant. The point of formulating the distinction in this way is seen if one considers any proposition as being of the form of a subject with a predicate attached to it. A proposition will then be analytic if the predicate is logically *contained* in the subject—as for instance "all bachelors are male," where the subject "bachelors" already contains in its meaning the predicate concept "male"; in the case of synthetic propositions this is not so, and the predicate is externally attached to the subject. It is at this point that we find the greatest difference between Leibniz and the philosophers who have used this distinction after him. Leibniz held that *all* predicates, except that of "existence," were contained in their subjects: he held that predication simply consisted of stating the properties which inhere in a substance. This might seem to destroy the distinction between analytic and synthetic propositions, because if all predicates are contained in their subjects, then all propositions will be analytic. But it is the exception, the predicate of "existence," that allows a place for synthetic propositions. On Leibniz's view, while it is a matter of necessity that a certain substance should possess a certain property, it is not a matter of necessity, and it is contingent, that that substance should exist rather than some other. His doctrine, therefore, is that it is impossible that a certain substance which has a certain property should not have had that property–in that case it would have been a different substance–but it is possible that some other substance might have been created in place of this one, which indeed had the other properties of this, but lacked the one in question.

This exception for existence is not an arbitrary postulate of Leibniz's. So different in fact are ascriptions of existence from ascriptions of properties that philosophers after Kant have said that existence is not a property at all. Leibniz does not himself take this view, and does consider existence as a property; but he could have put his theory of predication even more clearly and forcefully if he had anticipated Kant. This would, however, have been inconsistent with his view that there is *one* existential proposition which is not, like all the others, contingent, viz., the proposition asserting the existence of God: For Leibniz *does* want to keep an argument (shown in the extract from *The Ultimate Origin of Things*) to prove that there must be one substance whose essence includes existence, i.e., the existence of which is a necessary truth.

The question now arises, how can the properties of a substance change? For if the properties are necessarily connected with the substance, and it could not fail to have the properties it has, and still be the same substance, how do we account for the evident fact that things change, losing some properties and gaining others? Leibniz's answer to this is that the properties of a substance are, in a sense, eternal: that is, it is always true of it that it should have, at various times, the properties it does have at those times. This conclusion is in fact merely the consequence of a strict application of Leibniz's doctrine about predicates. In such a proposition as "Caesar is going to cross the Rubicon," " . . . is going to cross the Rubicon" is as much a predicate of Caesar as ". . . is crossing the Rubicon" is in "Caesar is crossing the Rubicon"; and so the same principle holds, that predicates referring to the future (and similarly those referring to the past) inhere in the subject, and are part of its nature. Each substance, according to Leibniz, is marked with its past and is "big with its future." The process in which one state of a substance follows on another Leibniz calls the "activity" of the substance (cf. *Monadology*, 22).

The action of an individual substance, which has been introduced in this way, is central to Leibniz's philosophy. A substance is something the name of which can *only* be a subject in a proposition, and cannot be predicated of anything: the word "I" refers to such a substance. This substance is also that which persists through any change; it is the same "I" who now does one thing and now another; and therefore it cannot be the things I do, or the things that happen to me, or the thoughts I have, that make up the real "I": all these things are predicated of the "I," which must be something behind all these. This Leibniz explains in the third extract, from *Identity in Individuals and in Propositions*. . . . Hence we have the doctrine that substances are timeless or eternal; this is closely integrated with the doctrine of predication just mentioned.

It follows from these considerations that no substance can affect any other; for if all the properties of a substance are eternally inherent in it, clearly nothing outside it can bring about a change in them. But if this is so, how do we explain the causal relations which we observe between one thing and another? Leibniz answers this by postulating a *pre-established harmony* between substances, such that the changes that spontaneously occur in each of them are correlated with every other. These correlations can be detected and formulated in scientific laws; these laws will be contingent in Leibniz's system, that is, it makes sense to suppose that the correlation might have worked out differently. The doctrine of the pre-established harmony perhaps sounds gratuitous; but it both follows from the system and contains an important insight. Leibniz has seen some distinctions that were put very differently by Hume: that to speak of a causal connection as a kind of influence of one thing over another is to adopt a kind of imaginative picture; all that is in fact given in experience as the basis of causal connection is observed uniformities between events. But

Leibniz's doctrine is in one way more fruitful than Hume's, for Hume was concerned only with causal laws, but Leibniz is concerned with *functional* laws — laws, that is, that state not what causes what, but what precise mathematical relation relates variations in one thing with variations in another; and functions play a much larger part in physics than causes do. So we find Leibniz in a passage from the *Discourse on Metaphysics* explaining what he means in terms of finding an equation for the line drawn through any arbitrarily selected set of points.

2. *The Principle of Sufficient Reason.* In this last example. Leibniz has given something that characteristically illuminates his thought. It can be proved that a function can be found to fit any line drawn through any set of points: but the function will be of greater or less complexity, depending on how regular the arrangement of the points is. Leibniz has a principle which governs the nature of the functions and of the laws which fit what actually happens: one will always find in explaining the world in this way a combination of the *greatest simplicity with the greatest diversity.* This is one formulation of the *Principle of Sufficient Reason.* The principle of non-contradiction constitutes a general test for truths of reason, the principle of sufficient reason constitutes a general test for truths of fact. It is established in Leibniz's system that whether a particular substance exists, having certain properties, is a matter of contingent fact; it is not self-contradictory to suppose that different ones might have existed instead. It has also been shown that, since it is a contingent fact that certain substances exist with certain properties, the laws which state a correlation between the properties of different substances must be contingent truths. We now want to know why just *these* substances exist, and just *these* laws are true: it is this question that the principle of sufficient reason is designed to answer. It states that, for every contingent truth, a reason or cause can be given, why it should be so; there is an overruling principle in accordance with which all things come about, viz., the requirements of "good order, and perfection." God had an infinity of worlds to choose from in creating. He must have chosen,

on Leibniz's view, that which is the most perfect, and that which has the greatest diversity of contents arranged in the most economical manner. This principle has for Leibniz a moral significance, which will be considered later; but he employs it widely as a logical or methodological postulate, and it seems to express the requirement that a scientific hypothesis or explanation should combine so far as possible simplicity with breadth and fruitfulness of explanation. A particular application of the principle is to be found in Leibniz's principle of continuity—that "Nature never makes leaps."

Is the principle of sufficient reason itself necessary or contingent? It might seem that, at least in the form in which it can be used to explain what actually and contingently happens, it must be contingent; for if it were necessary, then it would be a matter of necessity that certain contingent laws of nature should hold; and then it would seem that the laws of nature would have to be both necessary and contingent, which is absurd. Again, God has a free choice of what world to create; and for this to be so (as will be seen later) the principle on which He chooses must be contingent. Nevertheless the question is not as simple as this; for there is at least one form of the principle which is necessary, viz., that which states that there must be *some* reason for everything. About this it can be said (as Bertrand Russell has said in his admirable book on Leibniz) that there are two forms of the principle: the general, which just postulates *some* reason, applies to possible worlds and is necessary, and the particular, which postulates a certain kind of reason (the requirement of order, perfection, and good), applies to the actual world, and is contingent.

But it is not clear that this solution is correct. In the essay on *The Ultimate Nature of Things* Leibniz argues from the contingent nature of things in the world to the existence of a necessary being. Without God, he argues, nothing could be explained at all; all explanations would be left hanging in the air, incomplete, if there were no necessary being who was the reason for them all. He further states that it must be possible in principle to argue downwards from the nature of God to what must be the case in the world; ultimately one gets to particulars, which, because they each have an infinite number of properties, must be incomprehensible except to an infinite mind. This last consideration certainly leaves contingency in the knowledge of particulars, at least so far as finite minds are concerned; but above that level it may be that Leibniz had some idea that contingencies could be seen as necessities if –what he considered in fact impossible–we succeeded in deducing the whole system of natural laws from the perfection of God.

3. *The Identity of Indiscernibles.* By the principle of sufficient reason in its particular application, God has arranged for the greatest possible diversity in the world; and from this it follows that no two substances can have all their properties in common. If two substances were to have all their properties in common, i.e., were indiscernible, they would be identical, i.e., not two substances at all, but one. This principle is known as that of the *Identity of Indiscernibles.*

Again, it is not entirely clear whether Leibniz regarded this principle as contingent or necessary. In general he seems to have thought it contingent; logically, it could be otherwise, but actually it would not be, because God would not so choose. Yet there are some grounds for thinking it to be necessary. First, in his remarks on Newton's *Principles* he refers to the idea of two indiscernible universes as an *impossible* fiction; and impossibility in Leibniz generally means metaphysical or logical impossibility. Second, he supports the principle by a different appeal to the principle of Sufficient Reason–that God could have had no reason for choosing between two indiscernible substances in choosing what to create. But God chooses between what is possible, not what is actual; the actual is what he has in fact chosen. So this argument must mean that there could not be two *possible* indiscernibles, and not just that there could not be two actual ones. But from this it follows that two indiscernibles are not even possible, and hence, by all Leibniz's doctrines about necessity, that the Indentity of Indiscernibles is a necessary truth.

However this may be, there is one clear and important

feature of the doctrine that must be noted: the differences in place and time are not included in the differences required to make two substances discernible. It may be easily agreed that there cannot be two things in the same place at the same time; but Leibniz's requirement is more stringent—that even at different places, or at different times, there cannot be two things which are exactly alike. Leibniz believed this because of his doctrines of time and space; he held against Newton, that these were relative. and were themselve only to be explained in terms of the relations between particulars, which accordingly had to be distinguished without reference to space and time.

[*Logic and the Foundations of the Sciences. The Principle of Sufficient Reason.*

There are two basic principles of all reasonings, the principle of contradiction . . . and the principle that a reason must be given. i.e., that every true proposition which is not known to be so per se, has an a priori proof, or that for every truth a reason can be given. or, in the common phrase that nothing happens without a cause Arithmetic and Geometry do not need the latter principle but Physics and Mechanics do, and Archimedes employed it. . . .

I use two principle in demonstration one that whatever implies a contradiction is false, the other that a reason can be given for every truth that is not immediate or a statement of an identity that is that the concept of the predicate is always explicitly or implicitly contained in the concept of its subject. and that this holds good no less in extrinsic than in intrinsic denominations, no less in contingent than in necessary truths . . .

As there is an infinity of possible worlds, there is also an infinity of laws, some of which are proper to one and others to another and each possible individual of any world contains in its own notion the laws of its world. . . .

I think you will concede that not everything that is possible exists. . . . But when this is admitted, it follows that it is not from absolute necessity but from some other reason (such as good order, perfection) that some possibles obtain existence rather than others.

Identity in Individuals and true Propositions (1686)

Let a certain straight line A B C represent a certain time, and let a certain individual, say myself, endure or exist during this period. Then let us consider the me that exists during the time A B and the me that exists during the time B C. Since we suppose that it is the same individual substance that persists in me during the time A B while I am in Paris and the time B C while I am in Germany, there must be some reason for our truly saying that I persist, or that it is the same I who was in Paris and is now in Germany; if there were no reason, then it would be correct to say it was not I but another person. Certainly I am convinced a posteriori of this identity, from introspection, but there must also be some a priori reason. The only reason that can be found is the fact that the attributes of the preceding time and state and the attributes of the succeeding time and state are all predicates of the same subject [*insunt eodem subjecto*]. Now, what is it to say that the predicate is in the subject, if not that the concept of the predicate is in some manner involved in the concept of the subject? Since from the moment that I began to exist it could be truly said of me that this or that would happen to me, we must allow that the predicates in question are principles involved in the subject or in the complete concept of me, which constitutes what is called the ego and is the basis of the interconnection of all my different states. These have been known to God from all eternity. . . . When I say that the individual concept of Adam entails all that will ever happen to him, I mean no more than what philosophers understand when they say of a true proposition that the predicate is contained in the subject. . . .

I consider a true proposition as such that every predicate, necessary or contingent, past, present or future, is contained in the concept of the subject. . . . This is a very important proposition which ought to be well established, for it follows from it that every soul is as a world apart, independent of everything else except God; that the soul is not only immortal and impenetrable, but retains in its sub-

stance traces of everything that happens to it. This proposition also determines the nature of the relations and
communication between substances and, in particular. the
union of the soul and body. The latter is not explained by
the ordinary hypothesis that one physically influences the
other; rather each present state of a subject occurs in it
spontaneously, and is nothing but a consequence of its
preceding state. Nor does the hypothesis of occasional
causes explain, as Descartes and his followers imagine . . .
My hypothesis of concomitant harmony seems to me to
show how it happens. That is to say, every substance
expresses the whole sequence of the universe in accordance
with its own view-point or relationship to the rest, so that
all are in perfect correspondence with one another.

On Newton's Mathematical Principles of Philosophy

5. These great principles of a sufficient reason and of
the identity of indiscernibles change the state of metaphysics. That science becomes real and demonstrative by
means of these principles; before it generally consisted of
empty words.

6. To suppose two things indiscernible, is to suppose the
same thing under two names. Therefore to suppose that
the universe could have had another position of time and
place than it actually had, and yet that all the parts of
the universe should have had the same relation among
themselves as that which they actually have, such a supposition, I say, is an impossible fiction.

.   .   .   .

There are necessities that ought to be admitted. For we
must distinguish between an absolute and an hypothetical
necessity, and also between a necessity that is so because
the opposite implies a contradiction (which is called logical, metaphysical or mathematical necessity). and a necessity that is moral, whereby a wise being chooses the
best, and every mind follows the strongest inclination.

5. Hypothetical necessity is that which the supposition or
hypothesis of God's foresight and preordination imposes
on future contingents. This must be admitted, unless we

deny, as the Socinians do, God's foreknowledge of future contingents and his providence which regulates and governs every particular thing.

6. But neither the foreknowledge nor the preordination derogate from liberty. For God being moved by his supreme reason to choose, among many series of possible things or worlds, the one in which free creatures should make such or such resolutions (though not without his concourse), has thereby rendered every event certain and determined once for all; but he has not derogated thereby from the liberty of those creatures: that simple decree or choice did not change, but only actualised, their free natures, which he saw in his ideas.

7. Neither does moral necessity derogate from liberty. For when a wise being, and especially God, who has supreme wisdom, chooses what is best, he is not on that account less free: on the contrary, not to be hindered from acting in the best manner on that account is the most perfect liberty. And when anyone else chooses according to the most apparent and the most strongly inclining good, he imitates therein the liberty of a truly wise being as far as he is able. Without this, the choice would be a blind chance.

8. But the good, either true or apparent, that is to say the motive, inclines without necessitating; that is, without imposing an absolute necessity. For when God (for instance) chooses the best, what he does not choose, although less perfect, is nevertheless possible. If what he chose were absolutely necessary, any alternative to it would be impossible: which is against the hypothesis. God chooses among possibles, that is among many ways of which none implies a contradiction.

9. To say, on the other hand, that God can only choose what is best; and to infer from this that what he does not choose is impossible; this, I say, is a confusion of terms; it is mixing up power and will, metaphysical necessity and moral necessity, essences and existences. For what is necessary is so by its essence, as the opposite implies a contradiction; but a contingent thing that exists owes its existence to the principle of what is best, which is a sufficient reason for the existence of things. Therefore I say that

motives incline without necessitating; and that in contingent things there is a certainty and infallibility, but not an absolute necessity.

10. This moral necessity is a good thing, consistent with the divine perfection, and with the great principle or ground of existence, which is the need of a sufficient reason: whereas absolute and metaphysical necessity depends upon the other great principle of our reasoning, viz., that of essences, that is the principle of identity or contradiction: for when something is absolutely necessary, it is the only possible way, and its contrary implies a contradiction.

89. The harmony, or correspondence, between the soul and the body, is not a perpetual miracle; but the effect or consequence of an original miracle which was worked at the creation of things; as all natural things are. Certainly it is a perpetual wonder, as many natural things are.

90. The phrase pre-established harmony is a term of art, I confess; but it is not a phrase without content, since it is explained very intelligibly.

91. The nature of every simple substance, soul, or true monad, is such that each subsequent state is a consequence of the preceding one; in this lies the cause of the harmony. For God needs only to make a simple substance once to be from the beginning a representation of the universe, according to its point of view; it follows from this alone that it will be so perpetually, and that all simple substances will always have a harmony among themselves, because they always represent the same universe.

92. The soul, on my view, does not disturb the laws of the body, nor the body those of the soul; the soul and body only agree together; the one acting freely, according to the rules of final causes, and the other acting mechanically, according to the rules of efficient causes. But this does not derogate from the liberty of our souls; for every agent that acts according to final causes is free, though it happens to agree with an agent acting only by efficient causes without knowledge, or mechanically; because God, foreseeing what the free cause would do, from the beginning regulated the machine in such manner that it could not fail to agree with that free cause.

Reflections on Knowledge, Truth and Ideas

We insist here on a distinction between nominal definitions, which contain only characters by which we can distinguish one thing from another, and real definitions, from
which the possibility of things can be demonstrated. So we
may refute the view of Hobbes, who held that all truths are
arbitrary because they depend on nominal definitions: for
he did not recognise that the reality of a definition is not a
matter of our choice, and that we cannot consistently connect together any concepts we like. Finally, all this makes
clear the distinction between true and false ideas. An idea
is true if what it represents is possible; false if the representation contains a contradiction. The possibility of a
thing, however, is known either a priori or a posteriori.
It is known a priori, when we analyse the idea into its elements (that is, into other ideas whose possibility is already
known) and establish that it contains nothing incompatible.
For example, this is the case when we see the way in which
an object is produced, whence causal definitions are of such
paramount significance. On the other hand, we recognise
the a posteriori possibility of a thing when its actual existence is known to us through experience. For anything that
exists or has existed must certainly be possible. Wherever
we have adequate knowledge we have at the same time an
a priori knowledge of the possibility; that is, if we have
completed the analysis and no contradiction has appeared,
the possibility of the idea is demonstrated. Whether human
knowledge will ever attain to a perfect analysis of ideas,
and so to the first possibility and to unanalysable concepts
—in other words whether it will be able to reduce all
thoughts to the absolute attributes of God himself, to first
causes and the final reason of things—that is a question
which I do not want to discuss or to decide just now.
Usually we are content to ascertain the reality of certain
concepts by experience, in order then to combine them
synthetically according to the model of nature.

On the Ultimate Origin of Things

In addition to the world, or aggregate of finite things, we
find a certain unity which is dominant, not just like the

soul in me, or rather the Ego itself in my body, but in a much higher sense. For the unity dominating the universe not only rules the world, but creates and fashions it, is superior to the world and is, so to speak, extramundane, and is thus the ultimate reason of things. For neither in any particular thing nor in the whole aggregate and series can be found the sufficient reason of existence. Suppose a book on the elements of geometry to have been eternal and that one copy had been successfully made from another; it is evident that, although we might account for the present book by the book which was its model, we could never, by assuming any number of books whatever, reach a perfect reason for them; for we might always wonder why there should have been such books from all time; that is, why there should be books at all and why they are so written.

What is true of books is also true of the different states of the world; for although there are certain laws of change, a succeeding state is in a certain way only a copy of the preceding, and to whatever earlier state you may go back, you will never find in them a complete reason why there should be any world at all, and why this world rather than some other. Even if you imagine the world eternal, you are still supposing nothing but a succession of states; and as you find in none of them a sufficient reason for them, and as no number of them, however great, helps you in giving a reason for them, it is evident that the reason must be sought elsewhere. For in eternal things, even where there is no cause, there must be a reason which, in permanent things, is necessity itself or essence, but in the series of changing things, if it were supposed that they succeed each other eternally, this reason would be, as will soon be seen, the prevailing of inclinations, where the reasons do not necessitate (by an absolute or metaphysical necessity, the opposite of which would imply a contradiction), but incline. From which it follows that even by supposing the world to be eternal, an ultimate extramundane reason of things, or God, cannot be escaped.

The reasons which explain the world, therefore, lie in something extramundane, different from the chain of states, or theories of things, the aggregate of which constitutes the world. We must therefore pass from physical or hypothetical necessity, which determines the later states of the world by the earlier, to something which is of absolute or metaphysical necessity, for which itself no reason can be given. For the present world is necessary, physically or hypothetically, but not absolutely or metaphysically. That is, once it is determined that the world is to be such as it is, it follows that things must happen in it just as they do. But as the ultimate origin must be in something which is metaphysically necessary, and as the reason of the existing must lie in the existing, there must exist some one being metaphysically necessary, that is, whose essence involves existence; and so there must exist something which differs from the plurality of beings that is the world, which, as we have recognised and shown, is not metaphysically necessary.

But in order to explain a little more clearly how, from truths that are eternal, essential or metaphysical, there arise truths that are temporary, contingent or physical, we ought first to recognise that from the very fact that something exists rather than nothing. there is in possible things, that is, in the very possibility or essence itself, a certain need of existence, or, so to speak, a claim to existence; in a word that essence tends of itself towards existence. From this it follows that all possible things, expressing essence or possible reality, tend by equal right towards existence, in proportion to their quantity of essence or reality, or in proportion to the degree of perfection they contain; for perfection is nothing else than quantity of essence.

From this it is most evident that out of infinite combinations of possibles and possible series, that one actually exists by which the most essence or possibility is brought into existence. Indeed there is always in things a principle of determination which turns on consideration of maximum and minimum, such that the maximum effect is obtained with the minimum, so to speak, expenditure. And the time, place, or, in a word, the receptivity or capacity of the world may here be considered as the expenditure, or the ground upon which a building can be most easily erected, whereas the varieties of forms correspond to the commodiousness of the building and the number and elegance of its rooms.

It is rather like those games where all the spaces on the
board have to be filled according to certain rules and where,
unless some skill is employed, you will be in the end shut
out of some unfavourable spaces and will be forced to leave
many more places empty than you either needed or wished.
But there is a certain formula for filling most easily the most
space. Just as, therefore, if we have to construct a triangle,
and there is no further determining reason, it will be an equi-
lateral one; and if we have to go from one point to another,
without any further determination as to the way, we shall
choose the easiest and shortest path; so, once it is granted
that being is better than not being, that is, that there is a
reason why something rather than nothing should be, or
that we must pass from the possible to the actual, it follows
that, even if nothing further is determined, the quantity
of existence must be as great as possible, with regard to
the capacity of time and place (or to the possible order of
existence), much as tiles are fitted together in a given area
in such a way that it shall contain the greatest number of
them possible.

From this it is now wonderfully clear how in the very
origin of things a kind of divine mathematics or metaphysical mechanics was employed, and how the greatest quantity of existence comes to be determined. It is thus that of
all angles the determinate angle in geometry is the right
angle, and that liquids placed in heterogeneous media take
the form that has the most capacity, the spherical; but the
best example is that in ordinary mechanics itself: when
several heavy bodies act against each other, the resultant
motion constitutes, on the whole, the greatest descent. For
just as all possibles tend by equal right to existence in proportion to their reality, so all weights tend to descend by an
equal right in proportion to their gravity; and as here a
motion is produced which involves the greatest possible
descent of heavy bodies, so there a world is produced in
which the greatest number of possibles comes into existence.

Thus we now have physical necessity based on metaphysical necessity; for although the world is not metaphysically necessary, in the sense that its contrary implies a
contradiction or a logical absurdity; it is nevertheless phys-

ically necessary, or determined in such a way that its contrary implies imperfection or moral absurdity, and as possibility is the principle of essence, so perfection or degree of essence (through which the greatest number of things is compossible) is the principle of existence. From this it is at the same time evident how the author of the world can be free, although he makes all things determinately; for he acts according to a principle of wisdom or perfection. Indifference arises from ignorance, and the wiser one is, the more determined one is to the action which is most perfect.

But, you will say, this comparison of a certain metaphysical determining mechanism to the physical mechanism of heavy bodies, however elegant it appears, nevertheless fails in this; that there really exist heavy bodies, whereas possibilities and essences prior to existence, or outside of it, are only fancies or fictions, in which accordingly the reason of existence cannot be sought I answer that neither these essences nor the truths about them which are called eternal, are fictions. but that they exist in a certain region of ideas, if I may so put it, that is in God himself, the source of all essences and of the existence of everything else The existence of the actual series of things shows of itself that this is not just a gratuitous assertion. For since the reason for the series is not found in itself. as we have shown above, but must be sought in metaphysical necessities or eternal truths; and since what exists can only come from something that exists, as we have remarked above; therefore eternal truths must have their existence in a subject which is absolutely and metaphysically necessary, that is, in God, through whom those things which otherwise would be imaginary are (to use a barbarous but significant expression) realised.

Indeed, we discover that everything takes place in the world according to the laws of eternal truths, not only geometrical but also metaphysical; that is, not only according to material necessities but also according to formal necessities. This is true not only generally, with regard to the reason (which we have just explained) why the world exists rather than not, and exists thus rather than otherwise (a reason which can only be found in the tendency of the possible to existence); but if we come down to detail we see the metaphysical laws of cause, of power, of activity, holding good in admirable manner in all nature, and prevailing even over the purely geometrical laws of matter, as I found in accounting for the laws of motion; a thing which struck me with such astonishment that, as I have explained at great length elsewhere, I was forced to abandon the law of the geometrical composition of forces, which I had defended in my youth when I was more of a materialist.]

LEIBNIZ'S DOCTRINES RECEIVE THEIR FULL EXPRESSION IN the form, not merely of logical doctrines about predication, but also of a metaphysical system; the metaphysical system provides an imaginative picture of the structure of the universe from which certain conclusions are drawn about God's relation to man and human freedom. The extracts that follow show Leibniz's scheme of reality.

1. *Monads*. The logical doctrine of ultimate subjects provide a picture of the universe as consisting of numberless substances called *monads*. These must be (a) completely independent of each other—they "have no windows by which anything could go out or come in"; (b) they must be indestructible by natural processes, and could not come into existence except by an act of God's creation, and they have no parts; (c) they are unchanging, in the sense that their "activity" is the product entirely of their inner nature, which contains in germ all that will happen to them; (d) they are all different. Furthermore they form a system; not, in such a way, that they can affect one another, but they have been so arranged by God that the spontaneous activity of each in fact mirrors the whole of the universe, more or less clearly or confusedly, from its particular point of view.

The monads, Leibniz says, are the "real atoms of nature": but they are unlike the physical atoms of the scientist, and have no extension of any kind. Their inner activity Leibniz calls "perception," in virtue of its feature of mirroring the universe (i.e., the activity of other monads); the tendency within the monad to change these perceptions he calls "appetition." Everything consists of such monads; and so Leibniz has given us a picture of the universe as

consisting entirely of substances whose essence is, in some
sense, to have perceptions. But this does not make each
monad a *soul*, or every part of the universe animate; for
Leibniz insists against Descartes that there can be perceptions of which one is not conscious; this conclusion he
reaches partly by his Law of Continuity, partly by the a
priori consideration that the activity of the monad must be
unceasing, as there is nothing to start it off again if it stopped. Only those monads with memory and the power of
reflective thinking are properly to be called "souls" *(Monadology,* 19). In an early writing Leibniz had remarked that
body was "momentary mind, i.e., mind without memory."

The connection between soul and body is a connection
between monads: and therefore is not a *connection* at all,
but a case of the pre-established harmony. Leibniz was
very proud of this doctrine, which he opposed to the Cartesian theory of two interacting substances. It certainly contains some valuable insights: Leibniz was aware, for instance, that no amount of scientific investigation of the
brain could lead to the locating of perception or of thought
itself: (cf. the image of the mill, *Monadology,* 17). Leibniz's conclusions, are par excellence metaphysical, that is,
they assert that any adequate knowledge of reality must assume a certain form, which can be determined in advance.
He uses what would seem to many modern philosophers
quite different *kinds* of argument to make the same point;
for instance, as has been seen, the doctrine of the continuous activity of the monad is ultimately deduced from
a logical doctrine about the function of predicates, but is
reinforced by arguments from experience. By pure thought
we can anticipate the structure of science; and then we may
look in actual science for confirmation of this metaphysical
insight.

2. *Theory of Knowledge and the External World.* In his
New Essays, Leibniz criticizes the views of Locke, whose
Essay concerning Human Understanding (1690) had created a great impression. The extract from the *New Essays*
which is given below is concerned principally with the question of "innate ideas," concepts, that is, not given in expe-

rience; Locke had denied that there could be such concepts. Leibniz insists that there are; and his method of argument here shows his great philosophical subtlety. Locke had treated the question in such a way as to suggest that the existence or non-existence of innate ideas was an empirical matter, to be settled by introspection and research. Leibniz seems to realize that it is not an empirical but a logical issue; the question is—can all our concepts be satisfactorily reduced to, or analyzed into, concepts which are given in experience? But he adds the consideration that if it were an empirical issue, it would be undecidable, since one could not tell by introspection whether a concept had been given in experience or not. And this by itself shows that it cannot be an empirical issue.

Leibniz's objections to Locke go deeper than this; because of his theory of the activity of the monad, the whole distinction between what is given in experience and what is "innate" seems ultimately to collapse; in a sense, all the perceptions of a monad are innate, for all proceed spontaneously from its inner nature. Leibniz is here faced with a difficulty about the existence of the external world: if he starts from the Cartesian position of the existence of his own thoughts, it is unclear how he can proceed outside himself to establish the independent existence of number-less other substances; for, on his own thesis, these can never have any effect on him. To this question Leibniz gives no ultimately satisfactory answer. His answer is, so far as it goes, convincing: the coherence of observed phe-nomena, he suggests, constitutes an external world; that phenomena should hang together in the way they do is enough for us to say that there is a world outside. But this does not answer the question of how one estab-lishes the existence of other substances beyond the phe-nomena which appear to oneself. Here Leibniz has failed to give an epistemological answer (an answer to the question "how do we know what exists?") which measures up to his metaphysical answer (an answer to the question "what exists?"). This missing answer, Kant, who was deeply in-fluenced by Leibniz, tried to supply.

3. *Necessity and Human Freedom*. Leibniz had said that

everything which happens to a man is contained from the beginning in his essence; and therefore he was urgently faced with the problem of free will. If God had created a certain substance, say Caesar, who must by his nature act in a certain way, e.g., cross the Rubicon, how can it be that Caesar had a free choice when standing at the Rubicon? For, being Caesar, he could not have acted otherwise. Leibniz's answer to this problem is in terms of his distinction between the different senses of "necessary." One sense of "necessity" is that of logical or metaphysical necessity, necessity expressed in a truth of reason; the other is that of physical or hypothetical necessity, necessity expressed in a truth of fact. The opposite of a metaphysical necessity is logically impossible; the opposite of a hypothetical necessity is possible, but will not actually happen. The necessity by which a man acts as he does is of the second kind, for it merely follows from the principle of sufficient reason; it is a contingent matter that this substance, Caesar, who will act in this way, should have been created rather than some other substance. Therefore it is not (logically) impossible that Caesar should act otherwise than he does: although it is already fixed in his nature which way he will choose, he still chooses between alternatives, either of which is possible. Thus human freedom is preserved.

Leibniz, who is not free from self-congratulation, was evidently pleased by this solution; but it is hardly satisfactory. For the sense of "possibility" in which it is possible for a man to act otherwise than as he does, is merely that in which it *makes sense* to suppose that he does act otherwise, that this does not contain a contradiction; it is still an actual impossibility for him to do so. But if a man is gagged and bound, for instance, and is in this way prevented from stopping his house from being robbed, it still *makes sense* to suppose that he could have prevented the burglary: that he cannot in this case is just an actual impossibility. Yet no one would suppose that such a man was *free* to prevent the burglary. We need for freedom *more* than the mere logical possibility of the alternatives, which is all that Leibniz gives us. Yet Leibniz's treatment is not so easily dismissed: he is surely right, for instance, in argu-

ing that a man is still free in doing something which flows
from his character—that is, that the mere fact that one
could have predicted that a man would choose in a certain
way, because he was that sort of man, does not show that
he was not free in so choosing. This is a tangled and still
unsolved problem; Leibniz's doctrine is of value in drawing distinctions within it, even if he has perhaps not drawn
all that are needed, or drawn the main one in the right place.

4. *The Best of All Possible Worlds.* Leibniz's optimism,
his doctrine that God has chosen the best of all possible
worlds, became notorious. His views were violently attacked
by Voltaire, who in *Candide* represents the Leibnizian philosopher Panglosse complacently justifying God's choices
in the face of ghastly and meaningless disasters. Such criticism, though directed against a wilful parody of Leibniz,
has a point: for Leibniz's system, like all great metaphysical
constructions, embodies together with its arguments a particular view of the world, with moral implications, which
may be found either sympathetic or repugnant.

The comments on Leibniz given here have illustrated
only a few of Leibniz's doctrines and have discussed only
a few of the criticisms that may be made of them. It is a
tribute to his genius that proper criticism of him would
involve extensive discussion of all the leading issues of
philosophy. On all of them he held views still important
and fruitful, formulated in a system of such elegance, ingenuity and profundity that he stands as the model of one
type of systematic metaphysician and remains one of the
most suggestive philosophers of all time.

[*Discourse on Metaphysics* (1685)

VI. God's actions or acts of will are commonly divided
into ordinary and extraordinary. But it is well to consider
that God does nothing out of order. Thus what passes for
extraordinary is so only with regard to a particular order
established among created things; as regards the universal order, everything conforms to it. This is so true that
not only does nothing happen in the world which is absolutely irregular, but one cannot even imagine such a thing.

Let us suppose, for example, that someone jots down a number of points upon a sheet of paper at random, as do those who practice the ridiculous art of Geomancy; now I say that it is possible to find a geometrical line the concept of which will be constant and uniform, that is, in accordance with a certain formula, and at the same time such that it will pass through all these points, and in the same order as the hand jotted them down; also, if a continuous line is drawn which is now straight, now circular and now of any other description, it is possible to find a notion, a formula, or an equation, common to all the points on this line in virtue of which the changes must occur. There is no face, for instance, the outline of which does not form part of a geometric line and which cannot be traced completely by a certain movement according to rule. But when the formula is very complex, what conforms to it passes for irregular. Thus we may say that, in whatever manner God created the world, it would always have been regular and in a certain general order. God, however, has chosen the most perfect, that is to say, the one which is at the same time the simplest in hypothesis and the richest in phenomena, as might be the case with a geometric line, the construction of which was easy, but whose properties and effects were very remarkable and extensive. . . .

IX. There follow from this [the inclusion of predicates in their subject] several notable paradoxes; among others that it is not true that two substances may be exactly alike and differ only numerically [solo numero], and that what St. Thomas says on this point about angels and intelligences (quod ibi omne individuum sit species infima) is true of all substances, provided that one takes the specific difference, as Geometers take it in the case of figures; again that a substance can begin only through creation and perish only through annihilation; that a substance cannot be divided into two, nor one be made of two, and so the number of substances neither increases nor diminishes through natural means, although they are frequently transformed. Furthermore every substance is like a whole world, and like a mirror of God or of the universe, which they portray, each one in its own fashion; much as the same city is variously rep-

resented according to the various viewpoints from which it
is regarded. Thus the universe is in some sort multiplied as
many times as there are substances, and the glory of God
in the same way is multiplied by as many wholly different
representations of his work. It can even be said that every
substance bears in some sort the character of God's infinite
wisdom and omnipotence and imitates him as much as it
can; for it expresses, even though confusedly, all that happens in the universe, past, present and future, and thus
has some resemblance to an infinite perception or power
of knowing. And since all other substances express this
substance in turn, and accommodate themselves to it, we
can say that it extends its power over all the others in
imitation of the omnipotence of the creator.

XIII. . . . We have said that the concept of an individual
substance includes once for all everything which can ever
happen to it, and that in considering the concept one will
be able to see everything that can be truly predicated of the
individual, just as we can see in the nature of a circle all
the properties that can be derived from it. But it seems that
in this way the difference between contingent and necessary
truths will be destroyed, that there will be no place for
human liberty, and that an absolute fatality will rule over
all our actions as well as over all the other events of the
world. To this I reply that a distinction must be made between what is certain and what is necessary. Everyone
grants that future contingencies are assured, since God foresees them; but, for all that, we do not say that they are
necessary. But (it will be said) if a conclusion can be
deduced infallibly from a definition or concept, it is necessary; and since we maintain that everything which is to
happen to anyone is already virtually included in his
nature or concept, as all the properties are contained in
the definition of a circle, therefore the difficulty still remains.
To meet this objection satisfactorily, I say that connection
or sequence is of two kinds: the one absolutely necessary,
whose contrary implies contradiction, and this has its place
among the eternal verities, like the truths of geometry; the
other is necessary only *ex hypothesi,* and so to speak by
accident, and in itself is contingent, since the contrary does

not imply a contradiction. This latter sequence is not founded just upon pure ideas and the understanding of God, but upon his free decrees and upon the processes of the universe. Let us take an example. Since Julius Caesar will become perpetual Dictator and master of the Republic, and will overthrow the liberty of Rome, this action is contained in his concept, for we have supposed that it is the nature of such a perfect concept of a subject to involve everything, in order that the predicate may be included in the subject, *ut possit inesse subjecto*. We may say that it is not in virtue of this concept or idea that he must perform this action, since it pertains to him only because God knows everything. But it will be insisted in reply that his nature or form corresponds to this concept, and since God has imposed upon him this personality, he is compelled henceforth to satisfy it. I could reply with the similar case of future contingencies, which as yet have no reality save in the understanding and will of God, and which, since God has given them in advance this form, must correspond to it. But I prefer to meet a difficulty rather than to excuse it by instancing other difficulties, and what I am about to say will serve to illuminate the one as well as the other. It is here then that one must apply the distinction between kinds of connection, and I say that what happens in conformity to these decrees is assured, but that it is not necessary; and if anyone did the contrary, he would do nothing impossible in itself, although it is impossible, *ex hypothesi,* that this should happen. For if anyone were capable of carrying out the complete demonstration to prove this connection of the subject, Caesar, and the predicate, his successful enterprise, he would in fact show that the future dictatorship of Caesar had its ground in his concept or nature, so that one would see there a reason why he resolved to cross the Rubicon rather than to stop, and why he gained rather than lost the day at Pharsala, and that it was reasonable, and consequently assured, that this would occur; but one would not prove that it was necessary in itself, nor that the contrary implied a contradiction. In much the same way it is reasonable and assured that God will always do what is best, although that which is less perfect does not imply a contradiction. For it would be found that this demonstration of this predicate of Caesar was not as absolute as those of numbers or geometry, but that this predicate supposes the sequence of things that God has freely chosen and which is grounded in the first free decree of God, which was to do always that which is the most perfect; also in the decree that God made following the first one, regarding human nature, which is that men should always do, although freely, that which appears to be the best. Every truth that is founded upon this kind of decree is contingent, although certain, for the decrees of God do not change the possibilities of things and, as I have already said, although God assuredly chooses the best, this does not prevent what is less perfect from being possible in itself. It will never happen, but it is not its impossibility but its imperfection which causes him to reject it. Now, nothing is necessary the opposite of which is possible. One will be in a position, then, to meet these kinds of difficulties, however great they may appear (and in fact they have not been less vexing to all other thinkers who have ever treated this matter), provided that he considers well that all contingent propositions have reasons for being thus rather than otherwise, or (what is the same thing), that they have proofs a priori of their truth, which make them certain, and show that the connection of the subject and predicate in these propositions has its basis in the nature of one and of the other; but that they do not have demonstrations of necessity, since their reasons are founded only on the principle of contingency, or of the existence of things, that is to say, upon that which is, or appears to be, the best among several equally possible things. Necessary truths, on the other hand, are founded upon the principle of contradiction, and upon the possibility or impossibility of the essences themselves, without regard in this to the free will of God or of creatures.

New Essays on the Human Understanding

. . . The question at issue is whether the soul in itself is entirely empty, like the tablet upon which nothing has yet been written [tabula rasa], as is the view of Aristotle and the author of the Essay [Locke], and whether all that is traced on it comes solely from the senses and from experience; or whether the soul contains originally the principles of various notions and doctrines which external objects merely awaken from time to time, as I believe, with Plato and even with the Schoolmen, and with all those who take in this sense the passage of St. Paul (Romans, 2:15) where he remarks that the law of God is written in the heart. . . . From this there arises another question, whether all truths depend on experience, that is to say, on induction and examples, or whether there are some that have some other basis. For if some events can be foreseen before any trial has been made of them, it is clear that we must here contribute something of our own. The senses, although necessary for all our actual knowledge, are not sufficient to give us the whole of it, since the senses never give anything except examples, that is to say, particular or individual truths. All examples which confirm a general truth, however numerous they may be, are not enough to establish the universal necessity of this same truth; for it does not follow that what has happened will happen again in the same way.

. . . It would seem that necessary truths, such as are found in pure mathematics, and especially in arithmetic and in geometry, must have principles the proof of which does not depend on examples, nor, consequently, on the testimony of the senses, although without the senses it would never have occurred to us to think of them. This ought to be well recognised; Euclid has so well understood it that he often demonstrates by reason what is obvious enough through experience and by sensible images. Logic also, together with metaphysics and ethics, one of which forms natural theology and the other natural jurisprudence, are full of such truths; and consequently their proof can only come from internal principles, which are called innate. It is true that we must not imagine that these eternal laws of the reason can be read in the soul as in an open book, as the edict of the praetor can be read in his *album* without difficulty or research; but it is enough that they can be discovered in us by dint of attention, for which opportunities are given by the senses. The success of experiments serves

also as confirmation of the reason, very much as proofs
serve in arithmetic for better avoiding error of reckoning
when the reasoning is long. . . .

It seems that our able author claims that there is nothing
potential in us and nothing even of which we are not at any
time actually conscious; but he cannot mean this strictly,
or his opinion would be too paradoxical; for acquired habits and the contents of our memory are not always con-
sciously perceived and do not even always come to our aid
at need, although we often easily bring them back to mind
on some slight occasion which makes us remember them,
just as we need only the beginning of a song to remember
the song Also he modifies his assertion in other places by
saying that there is nothing in us of which we have not been
at least formerly conscious But besides the fact that no
one can be sure by reason alone how far our past apper-
ceptions. which we may have forgotten, may have gone,
especially in view of the Platonic doctrine of reminiscence,
which, mythical as it is, is not, in part at least, incompatible
with bare reason; in addition to this, I say, why is it necessary that everything should be acquired by us through the
perceptions of external things, and that nothing can be
unearthed in ourselves? Is our soul, then, such a blank that,
besides the images borrowed from without, it is nothing?
. . . there are a thousand indications that lead us to think
that there are at every moment numberless perceptions in
us, but without apperception and without reflection; that is
to say, changes in the soul itself of which we are not conscious, because the impressions are either too slight and
too numerous, or too even, so that they have nothing sufficient to distinguish them one from the other; but, joined to
others, they do not fail to produce their effect and to make
themselves felt at least confusedly in the mass. . . .

In a word, insensible perceptions are of as great use in
psychology as insensible corpuscles are in physics, and it is
as unreasonable to reject the one as the other under the
pretext that they are beyond the reach of our senses. Nothing takes place all at once, and it is one of my great maxims,
and one of the best confirmed, that nature never makes
leaps: this is what I called the Law of Continuity, when I

spoke of it in the first *Nouvelles de la République des Lettres;* and the use of this law is very considerable in physics. It teaches that the small always passes into the great, and vice versa, through the intermediate magnitudes, in degree as in quantity; and that a motion never comes about immediately from rest, nor is reduced to it except through a smaller motion, just as one never completes running any line or length before having completed a shorter line; although hitherto those who have exhibited the laws of motion have not observed this law, believing that a body could receive in an instant a motion contrary to the one immediately preceding. All this leads us to conclude rightly that noticeable perceptions also come by degrees from those that are too minute to be noticed. To think otherwise is to have little comprehension of the enormous subtlety of things, which always and everywhere include an actual infinity.

I have also noticed that, in virtue of insensible variations, two individual things cannot be perfectly alike, and that they must always differ by more than a mere numerical difference. This destroys the concept of the blank tablets of the soul, a soul without thought, a substance without action, a void in space, atoms and even particles not actually divided in matter, absolute rest, complete uniformity in one part of time, of space, or of matter, perfect globes of the second element, original, perfect cubes, and a thousand other fictions of the philosophers, which arise from their incomplete notions and are not admitted by the nature of things, and which our ignorance, and the little attention we give to the insensible, let pass. These cannot be tolerated, unless they are limited to abstractions of the mind—the mind insisting that it does not deny the things which it considers irrelevant to any particular enquiry, but merely sets them on one side. . . .

1. (Intuitive.) Primitive truths, which are known by intuition, are, like the derivative, of two kinds. They are either truths of reason or truths of fact. Truths of reason are necessary and those of fact are contingent. Primitive truths of reason are those which I call by the general name of

identical, because it seems that they do nothing but repeat
the same thing without giving us any information. They
are affirmative or negative. . . .

Primitive truths of fact, on the other hand, are the immediate internal experiences of an immediateness of feeling. Here it is that the first truth of the Cartesians, or of
St. Augustine, *I think therefore I am*, that is, *I am a thing
that thinks,* holds good. It should be recognised, however,
that just as the identicals can be either general or particular,
and that the one class is as clear as the other (since it is
just as clear to say that A is A, as to say that a thing is
what it is) so it is also with the first truths of fact. For not
only is it clear to me immediately that I think; but it is just
as clear to me that I have different thoughts: that sometimes
I think of A, and that sometimes I think of B, etc. Thus
the Cartesian principle is sound, but it is not the only one
of its kind. You see by this that all primitive truths, of reason or of fact, have this in common, that they cannot be
proved by anything more certain.

I believe that the proper criterion concerning the objects
of the senses is the connection of phenomena, that is, the
connection of what happens at different places and times,
and in the experience of different men, who are themselves,
each to the others, very important phenomena on this score.
And the connection of phenomena, which validates truths
of fact concerning sensible things outside us, is verified by
means of truths of reason; as the phenomena of optics are
explained by geometry. However, it must be confessed that
none of this certainty is of the highest degree, as you have
well recognised. For it is not a metaphysical impossibility
that there should be a dream as continuous and lasting as
the life of man; but it is a thing as contrary to reason as the
idea that the plot of a book should be formed haphazard
by throwing the type together at random. Beyond that, it is
true that, so long as the phenomena are connected, it does
not matter whether they are called dreams or not, since
experience shows that we are mistaken in the measures we
take concerning phenomena, when they are understood
according to the truths of reason.

The *Monadology* (1714)

1. The *monad,* of which we shall here speak, is nothing but a simple substance which enters into compounds; simple, that is to say, without parts.

2. And there must be simple substances, since there are compounds; for the compound is only a collection, or aggregate of simple substances.

3. Now where there are no parts, neither extension, nor figures, nor divisibility, is possible. These monads are the real atoms of nature and, in a word, the elements of things.

4. No dissolution of them is to be feared, and there is no conceivable way in which a simple substance can be destroyed by natural means.

5. For the same reason there is no conceivable way in which a simple substance can come about by natural means, since it cannot be formed by composition.

6. Thus it may be said that a monad can only begin or end all at once, that is to say it can only begin by creation and end by annihilation; whereas that which is compound begins or ends by parts.

7. Further, there is no way of explaining how a monad can be altered or internally changed by any other created thing; for nothing can be transposed within it, nor can any internal movement be conceived in it which could be directed, increased or diminished within it, as is possible with compounds, where there is change among the parts. The monads have no windows through which anything could come in or go out. Accidents cannot detach themselves from substances, or go about outside of them, as the "sensible species" of the Schoolmen used to do. Thus neither substance nor accident can come into a monad from outside.

8. Nevertheless the monads must have some qualities, or they would not even be entities. And if simple substances did not differ at all in their qualities, there would be no way of perceiving any change in things; for that which is in the compound can only come from the simple ingredients, and

the monads, if they had no qualities, would be indistinguishable from one another, seeing they do not differ in quantity. Consequently, space being a plenum, each part of it would always receive, in any motion, only the equivalent of what it had had before, and one state of things would be indistinguishable from another.

9. Indeed, each monad must be different from every other. For there are never in nature two beings which are exactly alike and in which it is not possible to find an internal difference, or at least one founded upon an intrinsic quality.

10. I take it also for granted that every created being, and consequently the created monad, is subject to change, and further that this change is continuous in each.

11. It follows from what has just been said that the natural changes of the monads come from an internal principle, since an external cause could not influence their inner being.

12. But, besides the principle of change, there must be a particular series of changes which constitutes, so to speak, the specifications and variety of the simple substances.

13. This series must involve a multiplicity in the unit, or in that which is simple. For since every natural change takes place by degrees, something changes and something remains; and, consequently, there must be in the simple substance a plurality of affections and of relations, although it has no parts.

14. The passing state, which involves and represents multiplicity in the unit, or in the simple substance, is nothing but what is called *perception,* which must be distinguished from apperception or consciousness, as will appear in what follows. Here the Cartesian view especially fails, since it considers as non-existent the perceptions of which we are not conscious. It is this also which made Cartesians believe that only spirits are monads, and that there are no souls of brutes or of other entelechies. They, with most people, have failed to distinguish between a prolonged state of unconsciousness and death strictly speaking, and have therefore agreed with the old scholastic prejudice of

entirely separate souls, and have even confirmed ill-balanced minds in the belief that souls are mortal.

15. The activity of the internal principle which causes the change or passage from one perception to another, may be called *appetition;* it is true that desire cannot always completely attain to the whole perception at which it aims, but it always attains something of it and reaches new perceptions.

16. We experience in ourselves a multiplicity in a simple substance, when we find that the least thought of which we are conscious involves a variety in the object. Thus all who admit that the soul is a simple substance ought to admit this multiplicity in the monad.

17. It must be confessed, moreover, that perception, and that which depends on it, are inexplicable by mechanical causes that is, by figures and motions And supposing that there were a machine so constructed as to think, feel and have perception, we could conceive it as enlarged and yet preserving the same proportions, so that we might enter it like a mill. If this were so, we should, when we looked around inside, find only pieces pushing one against another but never anything by which to explain a perception. This must be sought for, therefore, in the simple substance and not in a compound or a machine. Furthermore, nothing but this (namely perceptions and their changes) can be found in the simple substance. It is also in this alone that all the internal activities of simple substances can consist.

18. The name of *entelechies* might be given to all simple substances or created monads, for they have within themselves a certain perfection; they have a certain self-sufficiency which makes them the sources of their internal activities, and, so to speak, incorporeal automata.

19. If we choose to give the name *soul* to everything that has perceptions and desires in the general sense which I have just explained, all simple substances or created monads may be called souls; but as feeling is something more than a simple perception, I think it right that the general name of monads or entelechies should suffice for those

simple substances which have only perception, and that those substances only should be called souls whose perception is more distinct and is accompanied by memory.

20. We experience in ourselves a state in which we remember nothing and have no distinguishable perception, as when we fall into a swoon, or when we are overcome by a profound and dreamless sleep. In this state the soul does not differ sensibly from a simple monad; but as this state is not continuous and the soul comes out of it, the soul is something more than a mere monad.

21. And it does not at all follow that in such a state the simple substance is without any perception. That is indeed impossible, for the reasons already given; for it cannot perish, and it cannot continue to exist without some affection, and this affection is nothing else than its perception. But when there are a great number of minute perceptions, in which nothing is distinct, we are stunned; as when we turn round continuously in the same way several times in succession, from which there arises a dizziness that may make us swoon, and which prevents us from distinguishing anything. And death may produce for a time this condition in animals.

22. And as every present state of a simple substance is naturally the consequence of its preceding state, so its present is big with its future;

23. And as on being awakened from a stupor, we are aware of our perceptions, we must have had them immediately before, although we were unconscious of them; for one perception can come in a natural way only from another perception, as a motion can come in a natural way only from a motion.

29. The knowledge of necessary and eternal truths is what distinguishes us from mere animals, and furnishes us with reason and the sciences, raising us to a knowledge of ourselves and of God. This is what we call the rational soul or spirit in us.

30. It is also by the knowledge of necessary truths, and by their abstractions, that we rise to acts of reflection, which makes us think of what is called "I," and to observe

that this or that is within us; and it is thus that, in thinking of ourselves, we think of being, of substance, simple or compound, of the immaterial and of God himself, conceiving that what is limited in us is in him without limits. And these acts of reflection provide the principal objects of our reasonings.

38. The final reason of things must be found in a necessary substance, in which the variety of particular changes exists only eminently, as in their source; and that is what we call God.

39. As this substance is a sufficient reason of all this variety, which also is linked together throughout, there is but one God and this God is sufficient.

40. We may also conclude that this supreme substance, which is unique, universal and necessary, having nothing outside itself which is independent of it, and being a pure consequence of possible being, must be incapable of limitations and must contain as much reality as is possible.

46. But we must not imagine, as some do, that the eternal truths, being dependent upon God, are arbitrary and depend upon his will, as Descartes seems to have held. This is true only of contingent truths, the principle of which is fitness, or the choice of the best, whereas necessary truths depend solely on his understanding and are its internal object.

53. Now, as there is an infinity of possible universes in the ideas of God, and as only one of them can exist, there must be a sufficient reason for the choice of God, which determines him to select one rather than another.

54. And this reason can be found only in the fitness, or in the degrees of perfection that these worlds contain, each possible world having a right to claim existence in proportion to the measure of perfection which it possesses.

60. Besides, we can see, in what I have just said, the a priori reasons why things could not be otherwise than they are. For God, in regulating the whole, has had regard to each part, and particularly to each monad, whose nature being to represent, nothing can limit it to representing only a part of things; although it is true that this representation

is but confused, as regards the detail of the whole universe, and can be distinct only in the case of a small part of things, namely, those that are nearest or greatest in relation to each of the monads; otherwise each monad would be a divinity. It is not as regards the object, but only as regards the modification of their knowledge of the object, that monads are limited. They all confusedly strive after the infinite, the whole; but they are limited and differentiated by the degrees of their distinct perceptions.]

Recommended Further Reading

BACON

The Philosophical Works of Francis Bacon, edited by J. M. Robertson. London: George Routledge & Sons Ltd., 1905.

Works, edited by James Spedding, R. L. Ellis and D. D. Heath. London: 1857-74 (14 v.).

Selected Writings of Francis Bacon, edited by Hugh G. Dick. New York: Random House, 1955. (Modern Library.)

GALILEO

Dialogues Concerning the Two New Sciences, translated by Henry Crew and Alfonso de Salvio. New York: The Dover Publishing Company, 1952.

Dialogue on the Great World Systems, edited by Giorgio de Santillana. Chicago: University of Chicago Press, 1953.

HOBBES

Leviathan, edited by A. R. Waller. New York: The Macmillan Company, 1904.

Leviathan, New York: E. P. Dutton & Co., Inc., 1950. (Everyman's Library.)

Selections, edited by F. J. E. Woodbridge. New York: Charles Scribner's Sons, 1930.

De Cive; or The Citizen, edited by Sterling P. Lamprecht. New York: Appleton-Century-Crofts, 1949.

DESCARTES

The Philosophical Works of Descartes, translated by Elizabeth S. Haldane and G. R. T. Ross. Cambridge: The University Press, 1931-34 (2 v.). The most useful English edition.

A Discourse on Method and Selected Writings, translated by John Veitch. London and Toronto: J. M. Dent & Sons Ltd. New York: E. P. Dutton & Co., Inc., 1951. (Everyman's Library).

Selections, edited by Ralph M. Eaton. New York: Charles Scribner's Sons, 1927.

PASCAL

Pensées, translated by W. F. Trotter. New York: E. P. Dutton & Co., Inc., 1954. (Everyman's Library.)

Pensées and The Provincial Letters, translated by W. F. Trotter and Thomas McCrie. New York: Random House, 1941. (Modern Library.)

SPINOZA

The Chief Works of Benedict de Spinoza, translated from the Latin by R. H. M. Elwes. New York: The Dover Publishing Company, 1952.

Ethics, and On the Improvement of the Understanding, translated from the Latin by William H. White, edited by James Gutmann. New York: Hafner Publishing Company, 1949.

The Correspondence of Spinoza, translated and edited by A. Wolf. London: George Allen & Unwin Ltd. New York: The Dial Press, 1928. The best edition of the letters.

The Philosophy of Spinoza, edited by Joseph Ratner, translated by R. H. M. Elwes. New York: The Tudor Publishing Company, 1926.

Selections, edited by John D. Wild. New York: Charles Scribner's Sons, 1930.

Principles of Descartes Philosophy, translated by Halbert Hains Britan. LaSalle, Illinois: Open Court Publishing Company. (Religion of Science Library, No. 59.)

LEIBNIZ

The Monadology and Other Philosophical Writings, translated by Robert Latta. London: Oxford University Press, 1925. Includes *New Essays* and *On the Ultimate Origin of Things.*

Selections, edited by Philip Wiener. New York: Charles Scribner's Sons, 1951.

New Essays Concerning Human Understanding, translated by A. G. Langley. LaSalle, Illinois: Open Court Publishing Company, 1949.

Discourse on Metaphysics, Correspondence with Arnauld, and Monadology, translated by G. R. Montgomery. LaSalle, Illinois: Open Court Publishing Company.

Philosophical Writings, selected and translated by Mary Morris. New York: E. P. Dutton & Co., Inc., 1934. (Everyman's Library.)

The Leibniz-Clarke Correspondence with Extracts from Newton's Principia Mathematica, edited by H. G. Alexander. Manchester: The University Press, 1956. (Philosophical Classics).

Index of Names

186 INDEX OF NAMES

More MERIDIAN CLASSICS You'll Enjoy

(0452)

☐ **THE AGE OF REASON: The 17th Century Philosophers selected and edited by Stuart Hampshire.** Selections from the basic writings of Descartes, Leibnitz, Spinoza and other great philosphers of "the century of Genius," when science began to influence philosophical thought. With penetrating Introduction and interpretive commentary. (006988—$2.95)

☐ **THE AGE OF ENLIGHTENMENT: The 18th Century Philosophers, selected and edited by Isaiah Berlin.** Basic writings of Berkeley, Locke, Voltaire, Reid, Hume and other brilliant philosophers of the rational and humanistic age which believed that science's achievements could be translated into philosophical terms. (006996—$4.95)

☐ **THE AGE OF CAPITAL: 1848–1875 by E.J. Hobsbawm.** In 1848, the decisive defeats of the insurectionary governments throughout the continent opened the way to a period of political stagnation and economic expansion. Brilliantly analyzing the many facets of the age: commerce, industry, science, politics, art, morals, and manners, this volume offers an important look at a dynamic era that saw free enterprise at its most untrammeled. (006961—$3.95)

All prices higher in Canada

Buy them at your local

bookstore or use coupon

on next page for ordering.

Great Philosophers from MERIDIAN CLASSICS

(0452)

☐ **THE ESSENTIAL DESCARTES edited with an Introduction by Margaret D. Wilson.** A comprehensive selection from the writings of the 17th century thinker who changed the course of Western thought. Includes *Discourse on Method, Meditations on First Philosophy,* and *Rules for the Direction of the Mind.* (006759—$3.95)

☐ **THE ESSENTIAL ERASMUS, selected and translated with an Introduction and Commentary by John P. Dolan.** The first single volume in English to show the full range of thought of one of the great Catholic minds of the Renaissance. Includes the complete text of *The Praise of Folly.* (006732—$3.95)

☐ **THE ESSENTIAL ROUSSEAU translated by Lowell Bair with an Introduction by Matthew Josephson.** The major contributions of the great eighteenth-century social philosopher whose ideas helped spark a revolution that has still not ended. Includes *The Social Contract, Discourse on Inequality, Discourse on the Arts and Sciences, The Creed of a Savoyard Priest* (from *Emile*). (006740—$3.95)

All prices $4.95 in Canada.

Buy them at your local bookstore or use this convenient coupon for ordering.

THE NEW AMERICAN LIBRARY & COMPANY,
P.O. Box 999, Bergenfield, New Jersey 07621

Please send me the books I have checked above. I am enclosing $_____
(please add $1.50 to this order to cover postage and handling). Send check or money order—no cash or C.O.D.'s. Prices and numbers are subject to change without notice.

Name_____

Address_____

City_____State_____Zip Code_____

Allow 4-6 weeks for delivery.
This offer is subject to withdrawal without notice.

Exceptional Drama from MERIDIAN CLASSICS and
PLUME

(0452)

☐ **5 PLAYS OF THE ENGLISH RENAISSANCE edited with Introductions by Bernard Beckerman.** Encompassing the most extraordinary creative period in the history of drama, this volume includes: *Doctor Faustus*, Christopher Marlow; *Volpone*, Ben Johnson; *The Duchess of Malfi*, John Webster; *Women Beware Women*, Thomas Middleton; and *'Tis Pity She's a Whore*, John Ford. (006449—$4.95)

☐ **IBSEN: THE COMPLETE MAJOR PROSE PLAYS translated by Rolf Fjelde.** The first single-volume collection of Ibsen's major prose plays in chronological order. Included are *Pillars of Society, A Doll House, Ghosts, An Enemy of the People, The Wild Duck, Rosmersholm, The Lady from the Sea, Hedda Gabler, The Master Builder, Little Eyolf, John Gabriel Borkman,* and *When the Dead Awaken*. (254736—$12.95)

☐ **THREE GREAT PLAYS OF EURIPIDES translated by Rex Warner.** Violent love, brutal murder, pride, revenge, temptation, and virtue—these are the themes of the three great plays *Medea, Hippolytus,* and *Helen*. In his immortal dramas, Euripides has created magnificent character studies which probe deep into the hearts, minds, and souls of tormented men and women. (006724—$2.50)

All prices hgher in Canada.

Buy them at your local

bookstore or use coupon

on next page for ordering.

More MERIDIAN CLASSICS You'll Enjoy

(0452)

☐ **DEMOCRACY: An American Novel by Henry Adams.** With a Foreword by Henry D. Aiken. Vote buying and fixed elections, slanderous competition, preposterous graft—this is the Washington of the 1870s that Henry Adams reveals in his famous novel. The story of two people who aspire to power, here is an incisive exposé of corruption, in individuals and in government ... an entertaining caricature of government life that may be seen to have its application even today. (006511—$3.50)

☐ **SARTORIS by William Faulkner.** Foreword by Robert Cantwell and Afterword by Lawrance Thompson. A brilliant dissection of a decaying social class, and a vivid evocation of both the physical landscape and psychological climate of the South, *Sartoris* introduces many of the key themes, places, and characters of the Faulkner canon. (006465—$3.50)

☐ **THE SATYRICON by Petronius.** Translated and with an Introduction by William Arrowsmith. A classic of comedy, this is a superbly funny picture of Nero's Rome as seen through the eyes of Petronius, its most amorous and elegant courtier. *The Satyricon* is the hilarious tale of the pleasure-seeking adventures of an educated rogue, Encolpius, his handsome serving boy, Giton, and Ascyltus, who lusts after Giton—three impure pilgrims who live by their wits and other men's purses. (006538—$2.95)

☐ **A HAZARD OF NEW FORTUNES by William Dean Howells.** With an Afterword by Benjamin DeMott. A memorable portrait of an era and a profoundly moving study of human relationships, this novel centers on the conflict between a self-made millionaire and a fervent social revolutionary—a conflict in which a man of goodwill futilely attempts to act as mediator, only to be forced himself into a crisis of conscience. (006503—$3.95)

All prices higher in Canada.

Buy them at your local bookstore or use this convenient coupon for ordering.
THE NEW AMERICAN LIBRARY & COMPANY,
P.O. Box 999, Bergenfield, New Jersey 07621
Please send me the books I have checked above. I am enclosing $_____
(please add $1.50 to this order to cover postage and handling). Send check or money order—no cash or C.O.D.'s. Prices and numbers are subject to change without notice.
Name_____
Address_____
City_____ State_____ Zip Code_____
Allow 4-6 weeks for delivery.
This offer is subject to withdrawal without notice.

P

Quality Fiction from PLUME

(0452)

☐ LIVES OF GIRLS AND WOMEN by Alice Munro.   (254337—$5.95)

☐ MANTISSA by John Fowles.   (254299—$6.95)*

☐ THE ARISTOS by John Fowles.   (253543—$5.95)

☐ A BOOK OF SONGS by Merritt Linn.   (254329—$6.95)

☐ A BOY'S OWN STORY by Edmund White.   (254302—$6.95)

☐ ANIMAL FARM by George Orwell.   (254280—$4.95)*

☐ 1984 by George Orwell.   (254264—$5.95)*

☐ FLASHMAN AND THE REDSKINS by George MacDonald Fraser.
    (254302—$7.95)*

☐ CRIERS AND KIBITZERS by Stanley Elkin.   (250773—$3.95)

☐ FABLES AND FAIRY TALES by Leo Tolstoy.   (253020—$3.95)

☐ FANNY by Erica Jong.   (252733—$6.95)

☐ FEAR OF FLYING by Erica Jong.   (251060—$4.95)

All prices higher in Canada.
*Not available in Canada

Buy them at your local

bookstore or use coupon

on next page for ordering.

Ⓟ

PLUME Quality Paperbacks for Your Bookshelf

(0452)

☐ **FLASHMAN AND THE REDSKINS** by George Macdonald Fraser.
(254310—$7.95)†

☐ **THE HILLS BEYOND** by Thomas Wolfe. (253365—$6.95)

☐ **LIE DOWN IN DARKNESS** by William Styron. (253055—$6.95)

☐ **THE MASTER OF HESTVIKEN** by Sigrid Undset. (253837—$9.95)

☐ **SULA** by Toni Morrison. (254760—$5.95)

☐ **TAR BABY** by Toni Morrison. (253268—$6.95)

☐ **UNDER THE VOLCANO** by Malcolm Lowry. (251036—$3.95)

☐ **THE FOUR GATED CITY** by Doris Lessing. (251354—$5.95)†

☐ **THE GRASS IS SINGING** by Doris Lessing. (254825—$5.95)†

☐ **THE HABIT OF LOVING** by Doris Lessing. (252792—$5.95)†

☐ **LANDLOCKED** by Doris Lessing. (251389—$3.95)†

☐ **MARTHA QUEST** by Doris Lessing. (253535—$4.95)†

☐ **PROPER MARRIAGE** by Doris Lessing. (253101—$5.95)†

☐ **THE RIPPLE FROM THE STORM** by Doris Lessing. (251370—$3.95)†

All prices higher in Canada
†Not available in Canada

Buy them at your local bookstore or use this convenient coupon for ordering.

NEW AMERICAN LIBRARY,
P.O. Box 999, Bergenfield, New Jersey 07621

Please send me the books I have checked above. I am enclosing $_____
(please add $1.50 to this order to cover postage and handling). Send check
or money order—no cash or C.O.D.'s. Prices and numbers are subject to change
without notice.

Name _____

Address_____

City_____ State_____ Zip Code_____
Allow 4-6 weeks for delivery.
This offer is subject to withdrawal without notice.